WHEN LIFE GOES
TO PIECES

WAYNE DEHONEY

Cover design by The Author's daughter:
Becky Dehoney Richardson of
Vicksburg, Mississippi

FIRST EDITION, 2000
ISBN 0-9702395-0-5

Printed by

The King's
PRESS
P.O. Box 144
Southaven, MS 38671

INTRODUCTION

These sermons by Dr. Dehoney were preached at The Walnut Street Baptist Church in Louisville, Kentucky, during his pastorate there 1967-1985. Even though all of his Sunday morning sermons were printed and distributed widely among interested Christians, this group of sermons dealing with very practical problems we all face were selected to be bound together and made available for more people who appreciate Dr. Dehoney's preaching. Theologically sound and intimately practical, these messages will delight and bless again as much as when they were first delivered. Timeless words of truth set within meaningful personal interest stories and careful exegesis of scripture make these sermons eternally useful. I think it would be unlikely that Christians of many denominations did not find great value in what was preached. Very little editing was necessary because the originals were transcribed and typed so meticulously. To have helped in the process of bringing these sermons into your hands was extremely satisfying to me. I trust that your reading of them will be every bit as satisfying to you.

Ben W. Bledsoe, editor

FOREWORD

The Sunday Morning sermons which I preached from the pulpit of Walnut Street Baptist Church in Louisville, Kentucky were televised for 18 years and were also mailed out to over 4000 ministers and laity.

Mildred Snow served as my personal secretary beginning in 1954 and continues to serve in the year 2000.

She recorded, typed and revised all of my sermons for all of those years.

I would like to dedicate this book to her.

ABOUT THE AUTHOR

Dr. Wayne Dehoney is a Minister and a former President of the Southern Baptist Convention. He has been preaching for 62 years and served as a pastor in Tennessee, Alabama and Kentucky.

In 1985, at 66 years of age, Dr. Dehoney retired from the Walnut Street Baptist Church (originally First Baptist) of Louisville, Kentucky.

During his 18 years as pastor, the church built two multi-storied retirement homes with 409 individual units, a medical and nursing facility and several educational, recreational and family activity buildings.

With a combination of evangelistic preaching, innovative programing and creative social action, Walnut Street turned around from a declining inner-city church into Kentucky's largest congregation with 6300 members.

After retirement from the pastorate, he became Senior Professor of Preaching and Evangelism at the Southern Baptist Theological Seminary in Louisville, Kentucky.

Dr. Dehoney has been active in the Baptist World Alliance, traveling and preaching throughout the world. He has conducted evangelistic Crusades and organized Church partnerships to Russia, Ukraine, Romania, Kenya, Brazil and China. These missions have involved more than 3000 lay persons and hundreds of other pastors.

Dr. Dehoney is the organizer and conductor of the BibleLand Travel/Seminar that for 30 years has taken pastors and church members to the Holy Land. Under the auspices of Seminaries and Colleges, the tours offer academic credit for students and inspirational Bible Studies for all participants.

A prolific writer, Dr. Dehoney is the author and contributor of fifteen published books. His latest, "The Dragon and the Lamb" published by Broadman Press, is an account of the explosion of Christianity in the Republic of China.

Wayne and Lealice, his wife of more than 55 years, now live at Treyton Oak Towers, 211 W. Oak, Louisville, KY 40203. This is one of the Retirement Centers built on church property during his pastorate at Walnut Street Baptist Church. They have a son and two daughters. Dr. Dehoney has a great interest still in Dehoney Travel, of which his daughter, Kathy Dehoney Evitts, is president. The address is 1024 S. Third St., Louisville, KY 40203. Phone, (502) 583-1080; Fax (502) 583-2351.

CONTENTS

RECAPTURING YOUR DREAM

Exodus 3:1-6

One of the top NFL football coaches quit his job and went into obscurity. A reporter, interviewing him, asked, What happened to you? He said, I don't know — I guess — it is just burnout. I got to feeling sorry for myself and I got caught up under the pressures — and I am just burned out.

One of the major considerations in the church today is what they call burnout in the ministry. And we are establishing retreat centers and recovery programs for pastors who say, I am just burned out. They are ready to drop the ministry and resign a church — they are burned out.

Someone told me earlier about a friend that had been going to the same dentist since she was a little girl; and all these years she just thought all the pain and rough treatment was part of going to the dentist. One day she went to another dentist and was amazed at the difference. She said, I finally decided that he is just tired of his job — burned out — that is why he was so rough.

This word, *burnout*, is not a new word; and it is not a new idea. It describes an emotional experience when the pressures of life become too much and we just get wrung out emotionally. We burn out. It can describe a physical condition when the pressures are so great the activities are so many that we finally get burned out on the job and what we are doing. We do not have any energy or motivation to keep going. Or it is a vocational experience where we say, I have been with this same job, wrestling with the same problems, and I am just tired of it all. Burnout.

But it is also a spiritual experience. There is a spiritual burnout that comes to you and to me when we lose our vision, lose our dream, and lose the conscious presence of God. We lose the joy of our salvation and we get into the depths of burnout. We feel like we are just dragging along spiritually. It is just routine for us.

Are you one who has had a sense of burnout in your life — whether it is physical or emotional or vocational or, above all, spiritual? You do not have the spark and the fire inside you that you once had. You do not have the motivation and drive that you once had.

This story from our scripture text is about a man who burned out. But, one day recaptured his dream, and he went back to fulfill a role in human history that represents the turning point of the stream of humanity; and he was the leader of it. He did it after a devastating blackout in his life when, for many years, he lived in obscurity — burned out with his calling.

THE STORY

It takes place on the highest mountain of the Sinaitic peninsula. Jibel Musa it is called — the mountain of Moses. It is red granite, rising 7,363 feet above sea level — an overpowering sight. About 5,000 feet up is a vast plain of mountain meadows. Then, for another 2,000 feet, the rock juts straight into the sky. I have climbed to the top of that mountain — it is an exhilarating experience. I know this is the place where this drama took place.

Somewhere on those grassy mountain meadows an old Bedouin by the name of Jethro had pitched his tent. A wealthy old gentleman with many herds and many

2

flocks and much money. On a particular day, his son-in-law took his flocks to graze on the side of the mountain. As he went out, this old Bedouin said to his dark-skinned daughter, You did yourself proud when you married that man. He is a good son-in-law. Through all these years he has lived here with us, he has borne me grandchildren and I am proud of them. When I die — and it will not be long, I expect — he will get everything I have. He will be the biggest Bedouin chieftain in all this land. He had it made.

The next morning at breakfast, the son-in-law said, I am not taking the flocks out today. I am not going to take them any more at all. What are you going to do? He said, I am going back to Egypt. Jethro said, What! There is a warrant out for you for murder — that is why you ran away. I am going back.

Why? I am going back to lead my people out of bondage. But you tried that, and you were the son of Pharaoh then. You had power and authority. The people rebelled against you. They turned you in for murdering that taskmaster. They will not follow you. But I am going back, anyway.

Then Jethro struck that fatal blow — that one argument that comes to you and to me again and again. He said, It is too late — you lost your chance. You are too old. Your life is two thirds gone if you live the normal span of this day. You spent the first third there, the second third all these years out here — life is gone for you — you are too old.

That is what the devil says to every one of us. Your chance is gone — it is too late. Oh, if you had had a better chance when you were younger, you could have done it. But let the dream go — you are too old and it is too late. Moses said, Maybe so, but I am going back.

Now — what had happened to Moses that, in one 24-hour period, his life was turned around and he

3

marched straight forward into all of these obstacles and difficulties? Every argument that Jethro used was absolutely right. But Moses said, I am going back. What happened to him?

WHAT CHANGED MOSES?

We read it — the story of the burning bush. Moses said, Jethro, I was in the north pasture, coming around the brow of that cliff, bringing the sheep in — and I saw a bush on fire. Jethro says, What is so strange about that? Nothing strange about it — I just thought lightning had struck the bush. But — when I looked back, it was still burning. I walked a little further and looked back — it was still burning! A bush — on fire — that is not consumed. I whistled for the dog to round up the sheep and I stopped to watch.

When I moved toward the bush a voice called out, "Come no closer — take off your shoes — this is holy ground!" Jethro, it was the voice of God speaking to me. Jethro said, God! I thought you had quit your God. Yes, I had quit my God a long time ago — I quit Him because I thought He had failed me — but He had not quit with me! God never quits with us. We may quit Him — but He never quits us — He keeps on pursuing us. And now, at last, God speaks.

Moses answers, Here am I, Lord, what do you want? And the Lord said, Go back. I can not go. I will go with thee. Yes, but I cannot speak. I cannot speak to Pharaoh. Apparently Moses had some kind of speech defect — a stammer or a lisp. I cannot talk before Pharaoh, the mightiest man on this earth. I will give you a voice — I will send one with you — Aaron will be your spokesman. But — am I to ask him to let our people go? That is the mightiest army on the earth. Lord, I have no weapon. You have your shepherd's staff and I will give you power in that staff. It will be as a

4

sword. What you have I will use, God says. I have no army — no soldiers. But you have me. One man with a shepherd's staff in his hand plus God! Go and tackle Egypt.

That is a wonderful story of a man who caught his vision again — who dared to dream again — who recaptured his dream and recaptured his call. Late in life he found the will of God and did it. He marched straightforward into the face of the storm.

You ask, Can that happen to me? Can we recapture our dreams? Can we turn the pages back and get a fresh new vision of God — a new vision of His calling and what He wants us to do with our lives? Can we? God does not reserve these kind of miracles Just for the Moses', or the Jonah's, or the Elijah's. God is at work all the time — ready to come to common folks like you and me, ready to give us a new dream — a new vision. But we have to do what Moses did.

WHAT DID MOSES DO?

First, he had *an open mind*. He was open. He could have walked by without even seeing that bush. But he had an open mind that was curious — inquisitive — seeking. Is there something happening here? Can something happen to me different than usual? I am still searching — I am still looking — I am still open.

God cannot deal with a closed mind, whether it is 20 years old or 80 years old. If the mind is closed against Him, God cannot deal with it. Jesus pictures Himself as a shepherd standing and knocking at the door. The Bible says, Behold, I stand at the door and knock. But God cannot get in if we have a closed mind and a closed heart.

Do you go to church saying, My mind is open — my heart is open — maybe there is some great thing that

5

can happen.

Moses not only had an open mind, but *he also believed in the supernatural.* He believed in miracles. He believed things could happen to people. He was not turned off by the idea that there can be miraculous bushes that burn and are not consumed—that lives are changed and can be new again. He believed there was still a chance for the miracle to happen in this world.

You see, we live on two different planes. Some of us live down here at this physical plane. We say, It is all here — what you see, feel and touch — and that is all. That is all there is. There is no God really involved in this world. There is no divine providence working. There is only what we see.

And there are others who live at a higher level and say, "There is the great unseen world out here." There is a God who is on His throne — there is a God who is in every circumstance of life. There is a God who put you where you are — who controls the events of your daily living — who is at work in this world. He is a God of miracles who is constantly breaking through into the physical world to show His will and His way for men.

Moses still had that kind of an expectancy. He still believed in that kind of God, even though he had strayed far from Him. He came with an open heart and an open mind in a spirit of expectancy; and when he saw a miracle he was ready to say, God is here. I believe it. That is the way it can happen to you and to me. God is all around us. Even in the most mundane circumstances of life, God sets the bushes on fire for us to see. He shows His presence and His power.

Let me tell you a story to illustrate: most anywhere God can burn a bush if we will just be open to it. It was during the national finals for the basketball championship in San Diego, California.

6

One of our deacons who went had an experience that he shared with me. Those who were with Carl Kuhl remember the incident. He went to see a basketball game in the finals. But, as he passed through the hotel lobby he said, Lord, give me a chance to witness to somebody out here. I did not come just to see a basketball game; I want a chance to share Jesus Christ and my testimony. He prayed that prayer in his heart and in his attitude as he looked around to see an opportunity, to bear a witness. But the Lord did not seem to answer him. He could not find anybody that seemed to be open and receptive.

Carl went to his car to go to the game and it would not start; he had left the lights on. He went back to the lobby in a panic and asked the bellboy, Is there any way I can get service here — my battery is dead and I want to get on to the game. The bellboy said, You won't make it if we have to call for a wrecker. I have a set of cables in my car and I will help you. He pulled his car around — coupled the cables — and got the car started.

Carl said, You know, I was praying that somebody would help me — I just asked God for somebody — thank you, you are an answer to prayer, fellow. The fellow dropped his head and said, Well, thank you. Then, Carl said, Do you ever feel a need to pray to God and ask him to help you? You see how natural that was. Carl felt this was the answer to his prayer — somebody to talk to so he spoke to him.

Do you need to pray to God and ask him for help? Tears came in the bellboy's eyes and he said, I sure do —I am having a terrible time with our marriage — my wife and I had a fight and we have not spoken to each other in three weeks — I sure do need God to help me. Carl took his hand and said, You just look me straight in the eye and I am going to pray and ask God to help you. As I pray, you ask him, too. So like two friends

7

standing in the parking lot, like they were just talking from all appearances, he prayed:

Oh, Lord, help this fine young man to be reconciled with his wife — bless their home — may he open his heart and give his life to Jesus. May he confess his sins. In Jesus' name. With that he took his hands and said, The Lord bless you — now you do that. Carl got in his car and went on and the bellboy disappeared.

For two days, he looked for that bellboy. He wanted to follow up on it when they had time to talk. He had lost the opportunity, it seemed. Checking out of the hotel, he called for a bellboy. When he came, it was this same bellboy. Do not tell me God is not working in this world. Do not tell me there is not a supernatural spiritual power manipulating the events of people. That same bellboy — and he had not see him for two days.

When that boy saw him, his face was all smiles. I have been looking for you, sir. I want to tell you the most wonderful thing has happened. I have been saved and reconciled to my wife and it is just wonderful. And they knelt and prayed right there.

Now — that is a burning bush. God is at work in this world. If we will just be open — if we just believe in Him — even today God is going to set a bush on fire to reveal to me His will — if I can just see it. That feeling comes in our hearts — that yearning — that desire — something sparked there — and God is ready to deal with that. God is at work. Just as He worked with Moses, He is ready to set some bushes on fire today.

NEVER TOO LATE

Moses went back. And he would say to you and me, it is never too late to go back and recapture your dream. You are never too old. You have never gone down a road too far but that you can turn back. You can do it today! The world is full of examples of people who recaptured a dream and, even late in life, caught a new vision — a new life — a new beginning.

I am always thrilled with the story of Colonel Sanders. He was frying chicken in a little restaurant on a highway at Corbin, Kentucky, at 65 years of age when he started. He loaded an old pressure cooker in the back of his car and with a formula, a secret recipe and an idea, he went down the road and started Kentucky Fried Chicken. I have been all over the world. Whenever I say, Kentucky, they say, Kentucky Fried Chicken! Colonel Sanders! Do you know him? Have you ever seen him? And I pull out a picture where we are together. That gets me in anywhere.

But we can look right here: Taking the offering this morning was Carl Nussbaum. His gift of $650,000 made the Clara Nussbaum Children's Building possible. He was 55 years old when he started in business. With $6,000, he recaptured a dream and for the next 25 years, God used him and blessed him. It is never too late. Moses says you can catch your dream again — whatever it is.

Many times in Jackson, Tennessee, I stopped at the filling station operated by Paul Hardin, an elder in the Presbyterian church. He had the biggest business in town for service stations because he was so honest and zealous in trying to serve customers, in doing the extras, in going the second mile. One day Paul Hardin said, I am selling out and quitting. I am going into the ministry. At 45 years old, he came to Louisville Presbyterian Seminary and graduated — going out to serve as an associate pastor. He would say, It is never too late. If it is the will of God — if it is the dream that He has for you — see the bush burning today and get

9

going with it.

And you go like Moses — one plus God — and all things are possible! He stood before the mightiest man in all the world and defied the strongest army the world had ever seen. One man plus God! Moses led the children of Israel out of bondage and into the promised land, and he did it when, normally, we would say his life was already spent. — He was too old.

And I say to you: You plus God — and the world is yours. If it is His dream — if it is His will for your life — do it today! I cannot translate for you what that will is. I cannot spell it out for you.

It may have something to do with just coming back to church. You used to be so active — you used to be a deacon — the Lord used to be so close to you and you strayed away. You need to just come back and catch a new vision — get a new excitement. You may have taught Sunday School — you may have been so faithful — you may have been this and that — but it is a time to come back and say, I want the new dream. Recapture it. I want the fire to burn in my heart again.

Maybe you need to get your life planted in the church. You have been away — you just need to come back to that burning bush and say, Lord, warm my heart — I am going to put myself in the center of God's people here where I can get the joy of my salvation again.

If there is a crossroads where you stood years ago, and you took the wrong direction — it is not too late.

God says, Today is here and now. This is the day that the Lord has made and you, in this day, can start on a new path.

Whether it is like Colonel Sanders or Paul Hardin — whatever state you are in — whatever the direction is — you can start on a new life today. You can do it now!

10

DEFEATING THE GOLIATHS

OF LIFE

I Samuel 17:44-49

All the elements of a great story are here. Battle and conflict. An underdog, a despised redheaded, ruddy-faced, runty boy who had been rejected for army service when his elder brothers were taken. A giant who represents the forces of evil. Then you have the battle, and the boy wins!

This true story from the life of Israel is preserved for us to demonstrate how God can give the victory. How — as we face the Goliaths, the impossible mountains of life — we can win by faith in God.

THE STORY

So — we see the battle was stymied — 40 days and 40 nights the armies of Israel had been camped on the hillsides. Over there the armies of Philistia, and below, the Brook Elah, the valley of Elah. Every day this champion of the Philistines has come out and said, Send down the champion of Israel — let us fight hand to hand — and we will see which god is the greatest — the gods of the Philistines, or the God of Israel. And no one would go forth to fight him.

One day the shepherd-boy, David, came to the camp with ten loaves, some parched corn and cheeses for his brothers. He saw Goliath and heard him profane the name of God, and challenge the armies of Israel.

David asks, Why doesn't somebody go fight him? The soldiers, laughing, said, Boy, you don't understand!.... That giant, Goliath of Gath, is six cubits and a span tall! Nine feet, nine inches tall! A huge muscular warrior, and covered with armor from head to foot. His sword is as long as you are tall; his spear is like a weaver's beam — nine feet long. Even King Saul, who stands head and shoulders above other men, will not fight him.

David said, I would fight him. He hath defied the armies of the living God, I would go against him. They laughed at him— how would you do it, boy? About that time his brothers came up. Where hast thou left those new sheep? We know the naughtiness of thine heart — you came down here just to see some excitement — go on home! They are embarrassed and humiliated by the ridiculous proposal of their brother!

But word spreads through the camp and gets to the tent of Saul. There is somebody here ready to fight Goliath. Bring him in! Saul looks at David. You are no warrior — you can't fight Goliath. Why, thou art but a youth and he a soldier since his youth. You can't fight him.

David says, But, King Saul, I was tending sheep and the lion came against the flock. I slew him. Then a bear came at night and I slew the bear. The God that delivered me from the paw of the lion and the bear, will deliver me also from the hand of this giant. Saul said, Son, I guess you are right. What faith! You are the only hope we have! Bring him my armor. But the armor is so heavy, David cannot even stand up. David said, I cannot fight in your armor, Saul. I will go just as I am. My staff, my slingshot, a little stone.

So David crosses the ravine. There is Goliath sitting on a rock. Shepherd boy, you have not lost any sheep down here. Get out of the way — there is a battle going

12

on and you will get hurt. David continues toward him. Goliath says, I don't believe it — are you coming to fight me? He roars with laughter and shouts up to the armies of Israel, Am I a dog — literally, a puppy dog — that you send a boy with a stick to run me off? Get out of here, boy. I will feed your flesh to the birds of the air and the beasts of the field! Get out of here!

David keeps coming. He looks at that armored tank of Goliath — there was not a vulnerable spot on him. If David had come in Saul's armor — to fight Saul's way — with Saul's sword and Saul's shield — hand to hand, he would have lost.

But David came like a boy with a rifle against someone with a sword. And he saw his chance. As Goliath roared in laughter, and threw his head back, David could clearly see a spot in the middle of the forehead where the visor of his helmet went back and left his forehead exposed. David, with that slingshot, was able to hit the knot of a tree at 50 paces without missing. He said, God, I knew you would give me a way — thank you, Lord.

As he prepared a stone in the sling, David said, Goliath, you come to me with sword and spear and shield — but I come to thee in the name of the living God. The rock went straight to his forehead and knocked him down. David cut off his head — with Goliath's own sword and showed it to both armies. The Philistines turned and fled. The armies of Israel shouted in victory and ran them into the sea.

Isn't that a great story? God gave it to us for a reason, for a purpose. In it are elements of eternal truth that are universal. They apply to every life and every person listening to me today. It is the story of the victory of faith and the power of God at work in this world as we tackle the Goliaths of life! Faith is the victory!

13

I see some applications for us.

A CANAAN, A GOLIATH, A DAVID

I see in every one of us there is a Canaan; there is a Goliath; and there is a David — in every life.

First of all, there is a *Canaan*. The Philistines, the Hittites, the Canaanites and the Amorites have all occupied this land. But God said to Abraham, This is to be the land for your children. When these children of Israel were in bondage in Egypt, God said, Go out now and claim that land of promise. They marched through the wilderness and took Canaan. And God said, Drive out all the foreign elements. This is your land! You are to possess it, have charge over it, and be my people in it. They had driven out the Amorites, the Hittites and the Canaanites. But they had not won the battles over the Philistines; they were still there.

God has a Canaan for you and me— a promised land. That is the promise of life itself. When you were born into this world, God gave you a territory — This is to be your territory. I want you to conquer and claim it, possess it!

That promised land is the *potential* you have for everything you ought to be, and could possibly be, by the power and help of God. Your talents, your abilities are gifts and it is God's desire for you to be the best person you can be. Maybe it is a gift as a businessman, a singer, or a wonderful companion in a marriage relationship, a good husband, a good wife, a good mother. You see, this promised land, this Canaan, is God's dream for your life.

And then there are the many *Goliaths*. The Goliaths that come up against us are not just a great army. The Goliaths in our life are usually something singular. Satan uses that one besetting sin — that one weakness

14

that seems to get the best of us — the one thing that causes us to stumble so often. Maybe it is alcoholism.

Or a drive within us that causes us to violate the sacred seventh commandment. Maybe it is an inferiority complex — a sense that I do not count — I cannot do anything — a negative attitude about ourselves — low self-esteem. It is the one thing that stands like the giant Goliath and says You are defeated! You are stymied! You are blocked in life. You can't be what you want to be, and dream to be, and what God wants you to be!

Then, there is the *David* in us — the David, given of God. It is the David of faith when God puts his hand upon us and says, I will give you faith, I will give you power. You think you are so insignificant — but look at David — how insignificant he was. We think of David as king, the one who wrote the psalms. Don't think of him as what he became after this incident. Think of him at the time of this incident. He was the baby boy, the runty son — the shepherd boy. His three older brothers were famous soldiers — strong, good looking, handsome, with ability. All David could do was herd sheep. He was nothing.

What did it do to this young man's heart when the recruiter said, You three boys can come — you are fit to be soldiers. But, that runt, send him home to tend sheep. You would feel rejected — worthless — unable to accomplish anything.

When David came to the camp, his brothers jumped on him. What are you doing here? Get out of here. They scorn him. The soldiers laugh at him. You — fight Goliath? Ha-ha-ha! Then King Saul says, You are but a boy! You are nothing. And Goliath curses him. I will call you all kinds of foul names — get out of here — I will run you off with words. Now, that is how insignificant he was.

15

But God was in him. And the truth for you and me is that, regardless of how insignificant we may feel, how rejected and inadequate and inferior we may feel — God says, I have planted faith in you that has power to kill all the Goliaths of life, and to become my dream for you.

So — then, let's look at . . .

THE VICTORY OF FAITH

I find three elements in this story, and how this faith was made manifest in the life of David. First of all, *David had faith in the power of God* — not in the power of David. I come to you in the name of God, the power of God.

Jesus said, If we have a little faith, even as a mustard seed, we will be able to move mountains. We miss the impact of the statement of Jesus because we look at *quantity*. A mustard seed is the tiniest of seeds — yet a mountain is so huge. Here is the contrast: tiny and huge.

I think Jesus is also saying it is *the quality of faith.* Your faith may be so tiny, and the mountains so big — but they are changed because of quality. The mountain is just a physical material object. But the seed is a spiritual, dynamic thing that has God in it. When that seed is planted in the ground, it breaks forth with life and grows into a tree.

Jesus is saying — if you have a vital personal faith— not a hearsay faith or a secondhand faith — the very life of God is in you. You have been born again, and you say, God is real to me. You may feel like a mustard seed — so little — but God is saying, When there is life and my power, suddenly, that becomes bigger than the mountain — and the mountain shall be removed.

So, you have a little David with seed faith like this.

16

You have Goliath over there, a giant physically, militarily; he is equipped to win a battle. But, suddenly, the size is reversed. God is here, and God is not there. That is the difference — the quality of faith.

And notice *the reasoning of faith* that David had. David said, Saul, the God that delivered me from the paw of the lion and the bear, will also deliver me from the hand of this giant Goliath. Too often, our reasoning is to *unbelief* rather than *belief* — to unfaith rather than to faith. What do I mean? We reason negatively.

A woman lost her husband. She went through great sorrow and loneliness; but her son was still at home and cared for her. One day her son died and she said, Oh, what am I going to do? When my husband died, God gave me my son; he lived with me. But now, my son is gone — now I have no one. She reasoned to unbelief. When the husband died, why didn't she say, God help me. Now my son has died, God will help me — I don't know how, but He will.

We need to reason toward faith. The lion— God helped me. The bear— God was with me. Now, Goliath. I do not know how God is going to do it — I do not see what the chance will be — I know as I go against him, God will give me the opening. And God does. Faith in the power of God.

Then, secondly, *David had faith in himself.* Saul, I can't wear your armor. We go through life with people wanting to put somebody else's armor on us. Our parents want to put their armor on us — be just like us — do what we do — conformity. Life tries to put an armor on us. And some conformity is necessary for orderly existence, that is true.

But, David said, I can't wear your armor, Saul. And I cannot fight like you. I have to be me and fight my way. You know that song, "I want to be me"— there is some truth. We want to say, God made me like I am and

17

I ought to be proud of me. God loves me as I am; Christ died for me as I am; He has redeemed and saved me as I am. I want to be an individual — I do not want to rob God of the uniqueness that He put in me.

Students — how easy for us to pattern after other people and lose the uniqueness that God has given to us. Years ago at Southwestern Seminary, there was a professor of music, attractive and appealing. He had lost two fingers in a logging accident. As a result, he led the choir with those two fingers missing. He produced a whole generation of ministers of music who led the singing with those two fingers tucked under. They were unconsciously saying, I want to be like him— instead of saying, God made me and I ought to let God use me as I am. Do not ever depreciate yourself. You are God's unique creation. Like David says, I am going to be David, and face life with God's help.

Then third, *faith in God's purpose.* David did not say, I am going to win the battle for David — for Israel — even for Saul. He said, I am going to win the battle for God. He who sides with God is going to win. Mark that down. God will win. If you are not with God, you are going to lose in life.

What is God about in this world? He is at work in this world, in His church, in His body called the church, in witnessing, in changing this world. His spirit is loose in this world. If I align myself with God's ongoing eternal purpose, I am going to win. If I don't, I am going to lose. So — the battle is the Lord's! Remember, God will win — right now.

My Sunday School teacher died. I was a 15-year-old boy in Nashville; he was the son of J. F. Jarman, founder of Jarman Shoe Co. His name was Maxey Jarman. In his late twenties when I was a teenage boy, he influenced me greatly. When I got the word, I called Mrs. Jarman immediately.

She answered, Is that you, Wayne? I just wanted to tell you I love you all and am thinking about you. She said, Oh, everything is all right — God is so good. The Lord took Maxey home with Him and everything is all right. She was so buoyant.

She said, We live near a seminary and I have the boys working in the yard. The other day one said, Mrs. Jarman, you know God don't make no mistakes. And he doesn't, Wayne, and I know it. Everything is all right. Thank you, honey, for calling. Now that is the victory of faith!

And it reminds me of Pat Shaughnessy. He pastored a little church that did not grow much or do much. Then, something happened on August 6 in the Los Angeles airport that so changed his life that his church has exploded and he has been witnessing around the world.

Pat says, I was standing in the Los Angeles airport when a bomb went off. It killed three people —one beside me and two in front of me — and blew me 30 feet into the air. When I came down, I saw my right leg mangled, part of it gone. I knew I had lost a leg. The left leg had six fractures.

As I lay there, I thought, God does not have any accidents. God knew I was here — on the way to revivals in Korea. Suddenly, by the power of God, I became victor over what had happened to me instead of victim. I felt God saying, Pat, you won't understand — it is going to be hard on you — but I am doing something through you that will be wonderful. It will make you a greater preacher. And I will use you.

They gave me a 30% chance of recovery — but I got all right. The papers called it a miracle. My wife was driving me to the first service where I would give my testimony. In front of the coliseum she asked the traffic cop, Where is the handicapped space? I said,

Handicapped? I'm not handicapped! I still have my tongue! I can still tell about Jesus.

And Pat said, I realized I did not preach with my legs; I preached with my tongue. I did not need a right leg to preach. In fact, I preach better without a right leg.

Everywhere I go someone will say, What happened to you? How did you lose your leg? I lost it in a bombing — yeah, that bombing in the Los Angeles airport. Oh, yes, that's terrible! No, it's not terrible — it's wonderful!

Jesus Christ has given me the power to be victorious over this. I am happier and more successful today than I ever was when I had two legs. Let me tell you how Jesus Christ can let you be victorious over the problems in your life. It has opened thousands of doors for me.

That is what David said: The battle is the Lord's! Will you hurl the rock today, strike that Goliath and say, I will win the victory of faith today. The battle is the Lord's! Let Him have His way in your life!

WHEN LIFE GOES TO PIECES

I Kings 17:1-7

We have been shocked beyond measure by the terrible reports coming out of Africa where men, women and children are dying from hunger. And it is because of a drought, a climatic change that was brought about year after year without rain through that subsahara area of Africa. The tragedy of drought. The suffering of drought. The same kind of situation we read about in I Kings 17.

These were those kind of days in all of Israel. They had been three years without rain. Famine stalked the land — death was on every hand. The riverbeds were now just cracked dry gullies. What were once fields were now parched desolate desert. The skies were brazen, without a sign of a cloud — no rain. And it had all come about because of sin in the land. Elijah had appeared before the wicked king Ahab and his wicked wife Jezebel and said, Because of your apostasy and because of the children of Israel following after you and the gods of Baal and Ashtaroth, there shall be no rain in the land. Ahab had laughed him out of court — scorned him — and sent him on his way.

Now — three years later — it is different — for everybody except Elijah — he never had it so good, for God had said, You are my chosen one — you are my prophet — you are the faithful one — get thee out and go yonder to the east of Jordan to the brook Cherith. In that desolate desert area you will find a little spring breaking out of the mountainside — settle yourself down there — pitch your tent — and you will have water, and the ravens shall fly overhead and bring your food and flesh and you shall be cared for. And for three years Elijah sat beside that brook — life was never so good. No burdens — no cares. God provided for him — as God takes care of His faithful.

"If you walk with the Lord in the light of His word; Elijah said, this is what you get." And he sat there beside the brook saying, It is good to be one of the righteous chosen ones of God — how He has blessed me. He is so good to me. That brook was a symbol of God's goodness — a symbol of God's covenant and promise — a symbol to "follow me, be faithful, have strong faith in me and I will take care of you." There it was.

But — one day — Elijah went out to get a drink of water at the brook. He looked and said, That can't be. The water mark on the rock has always been so steady and so stable — it is a little lower this morning. But he drank of the brook and thought nothing more of it. He came back the next morning — a little lower. And the next morning — a little lower. One morning he came and found that the brook had dried into a trickle of water. Then came that terrible day — that awesome day when the brook went dry.

The brook dried up. That experience in life when adversity comes and it appears that every promise of God has faded away. Everything that seemed to make life good and rich and secure for us is gone. The brook dries up.

I was in a checkout line at the grocery store and behind me was a young mother with her little child about four years old. She was singing softly to that child the song Debby Boone made so popular "You light up my life." I could just see in her eyes and face all the love and joy and the fulfillment of life that flowed out of her. But what happens when the light of our life goes out?

22

A woman, whose husband had been a Baptist preacher in Oklahoma for many years, wrote me. She is in a nursing home and she said, I was so moved, and so many memories came back of my dear husband who died not long ago. She went on to talk about how the brook had gone dry in her life — the light of her life had gone out — the one she loved so much was gone now. The brook goes dry when the nearest and dearest one to us in life goes from us.

Prosperity and comfort and ease and success and the things that have made life comfortable and fulfilled for us are suddenly wiped away and the brook goes dry for us. When our dreams are shattered — when our hopes disappear — when health slips away from us and we limp along, crippled and weakened, we say the brook is drying up. Life is getting hard and adversities are coming upon me. And in all of that we begin to cry as did Elijah: Oh, Lord, where art thou? Where are your promises? Where is your goodness that you said should follow after righteousness? Where are you?

Isn't that natural? Isn't it more normal that failure comes more often than success? And want and need comes more often than wealth and prosperity — and sickness more often than health? Most of us have these low experiences of life when it seems that the brook is running dry; at least, it is trickling and almost dry. The light is almost gone out and we cry out, Oh, God, why?

A person said to me, Why did this happen to me? I have been a tither — and I have taught Sunday School and I have been faithful — and I have been good and tried to do my best — why has it happened to me? It is really a challenge as to whether God is there or not — whether His promises are true or not.

Elijah staked everything he had on God. He stood before the king himself and pronounced judgment upon the king and all the nation; and they were hunting for

23

him now and were ready to kill him for the curse he had brought upon the land. He had staked it all and God had said, I will take care of you. But now — God went back on His promise. The brook went dry.

Why did the brook go dry? I can give you some negative answers — some negative statements to explain it. The brook went dry not because God had forgotten Elijah. God had not forgotten him.

A dear person in a nursing home wrote with some bitterness, My children put me here — they have not been to see me in years — they do not care anything about me — they have forgotten all about me. Around our land there are forgotten people everywhere. Are they forgotten of God? They may be forgotten of family, loved ones, friends — but are they forgotten of God? I say to you, No — God has not and will not forget a single one of His children.

Jesus Himself said that God is so involved in our lives and so personally attentive to our every need that not even a hair from our head falls to the ground but that God knows that detail about our life. Not even a little sparrow falls to the ground but that God knows, so involved is He in every circumstance of life. He is a God of the detail and He knows every detail of every life. God has not forgotten you.

Neither can we say that God has ceased to love us. Jesus loves you, regardless of what happens in life. The brooks go dry and you seem so empty — adversity seems so strong and powerful and overwhelming — but God still loves you. He has not ceased and never will cease to love you. You may cease to love Him; but I tell you no person in this world has ever sinned against the love of God enough for God to say, I will not love you. You have not gone beyond the love of God. Regardless of what you have done, He still loves you.

Neither did the brook go dry because Elijah had

sinned. How often we say, Preacher, what have I done wrong? I must have done something terribly wrong in my life for God to let this happen to me. That is not necessarily so. Sin does bring suffering — wrongdoing does bring adversity and hardship and burdens upon us — but not all burdens and all adversity and all calamity and all tragedy are the direct result of sin. Elijah had not sinned and brought this calamity upon himself.

We have the simple answer in verse 7: It came to pass after a while that *the brook dried up because there was no rain in the land.* It dried up because of the natural law of God at work in the world. Some of the adversities that come in life are the results of the natural law of God in operation. God did not make these bodies to stay in this world forever. It is the law of God that this which is made of dust shall go back to the dust.

The loss of health and the aches and pains, the sufferings that come with it are a part of the process of the fleshly finite world in which we live. We are interlocked with the whole world; we do not live as an island unto ourselves, so the sins of other people sometimes spill over and bring hardship on our lives. We have not done anything wrong, but somebody did wrong and that chain reaction of sin brings suffering to us.

A line of cars is going along the expressway. Someone slows down. The driver behind that car is on drugs and his reaction is slow — so he rams the car. That car jams into the back of a car — that car is thrust forward and slams into the next one — it thrusts forward and slams into the next one. At the front of the line is a woman with her child. Her car is hit in the chain reaction and the child is thrown against the dashboard and seriously injured. You cannot say that that child's injury was due to the child's sin. It was due to sin, but the chain reaction of sin way back yonder

25

brought that about. That is a part of the law and process of the world in which we live. We are interlocked with each other.

But Elijah still says, Why did this happen to me? I recognize that there is no rain in the land — everybody is thirsty, but Lord, why did you let it happen to me? I am your child, I am your prophet. Why does it happen?

I can think of some lessons that Elijah learned while he was in the desert. He went to school to God down by the brook that day. And you and I sometimes, in the deserts of life, learn more by far than when life is blossoming and beautiful and lovely and carefree. The best lessons we learn usually are the lessons we learn through hard and difficult times.

So — the first lesson: *Trust in God not in His gifts* — water, food, things. Before we know it we are subconsciously shifting our faith to those things that we have; then, when we lose those things, we lose our faith. We must recognize that our security is never in things — our security is in a person — and that person is God, our loving Father. Sometimes He has to take the things away to get us back to where our faith is in Him.

I heard the testimony of a missionary family who was in the southern part of Africa during the time of revolution and terrorist activities. Guerrillas killed some of their neighbors and some of their black workers around the compound and burned their house and took all their possessions. They escaped with just the clothes on their backs. All kinds of mementoes, memories, things precious to them — personal to them — everything was wiped out and they walked away with nothing but their clothes and their life.

Their testimony was that this had caused them to discover that when they lost everything in life, they found the greatest thing — their faith in God — and how adequate and supreme that was, for it could cover every need of life.

That is what God has to do sometimes — take away the water and the ravens and things of life to make us realize where our security is. That is the first lesson in life to learn.

The second lesson: *Life is movement — life is action.* It is not a static situation where you can sit down and stay. I think Elijah would have stayed by that brook the rest of his days. Why move out? Why go on and do anything else? He never would have it any better than this. And sometimes God has to say, You were not made to stay where you are — life is to be a pilgrim's progress up and out and on to the greater things. I have to move you out and shake you up and pull you up. In order to do that, I have to take away some things in your life — I have to get you loose from here and get you moving.

What is God trying to do to you in your life? Have you settled down? Have you said, Lord, let me keep it just like this from now on. We all have that tendency, individually and institutionally. How easy it is for a church to just settle down and say, Keep it like it is. Do not change a thing. Just get somebody to keep house so we will not change it and it can be like this next year and ten years and a hundred years from now — I like it so well. God has to shake us up sometimes.

I went to preach a number of years ago at the First Baptist Church of Enterprise, Alabama. In the town square there was a monument to the boll weevil. I was told that in 1915 the boll weevil devastated Coffee County. The economy of this rich land that produced cotton made wealthy farmers out of everybody and they were just wiped out. It was a disaster. That is when they said, We must diversify. Now they grow peanuts and soybeans and prosperity has returned to this land. So, the citizens of Coffee County erected a

27

monument to the boll weevil saying, Thank God for the boll weevil — it shook us up and got us loose from our old ways and caused us to move out into a new prosperity.

Sometimes the boll weevils of life have to come and work on you and me for God to get us out of our patterns and get us to moving on to a higher level of life.

A third lesson that Elijah learned here: *He must turn the interest of his life away from himself to outside* himself. He had been looking at himself and saying, Feed me, I am enjoying it so much — Lord, Just keep on pouring the food to me — I like it.

God is saying it is time now for you to go out and start *blessing someone else.* You have been blessed enough. Take your life now and start using your life to bless somebody else. There are widows out there that are hungry — there are children that are starving and I want you to get out there and help them. Then I want you to help your whole nation. Get to work and serve the Lord. Start being a blessing to someone else.

Sometimes the light of our life is taken away from us so that we can shed our light of love in other directions to bless other people. In a missionary dedication service in Richmond I heard the testimony of a couple that was returning to the mission field after two years as journeymen.

They said, We are going back to the mission field because we had a little girl born into our family. She was the love of our life, but she died at 18 months, and the doctor has said we cannot have any more children. As we have worked through this terrible tragedy, we realized that God gave us little Kathy for 18 months to show us how much we could love a child. When we went out as missionary journeymen, we saw the hundreds and hundreds of little children that needed love. God

28

gave us Kathy for 18 months and then took her to be with Him to call us to love the children of the world and to go as missionaries to them.

You see sometimes God has to dry up the brook and put out the light of our life in order to get us to serve and share with others the love that we know in Jesus Christ.

I think there is yet another lesson. *The burdens and adversities of life make us strong — make us vigorous— make us develop and grow.* The grandfather clock had been ticking away for thirty years with two huge weights hung on double chains. The old clock said to the master of the house, I am so weary and so tired of these weights — I have to bear these weights all day, every day, week in, week out, year in, year out — please sir, take away my weights and let me be free of them.

So the master of the house took the weights away. Then the clock said, Oh, sir, I made a mistake. Give me back my weights.

The weights are what keep me going.

Now — I ask you, folks, aren't the weights of life what keep most of us going? Oh, I would like to be free from this heavy responsibility. But — take away that responsibility and I find I do not have the power to go — I do not have the power to rise up and do what I ought to do. Take away the burden that has been cast upon me. But — that is what has made me what I am! So, Elijah learned out there by that brookside that he needed some weights back on his life.

The simple application for you and for me: How can we put life back together again when it has gone to pieces — when the brook has dried up, when the lights have gone out? Just these simple words: *Do not be bitter.* That is the poison of the devil that he will pump

29

into your life if he can. You can wallow in your bitterness and stew in the juices of hostility and resentment and complaint, and you can share that bitterness with everybody to where they will back off and not want to be around you at all. Do not be bitter.

And, *do not quit.* Do not give up. Keep going. Learn from Jesus. Jesus took up the cross, not to let it defeat Him, but to overcome the cross and to use it as an instrument of victory and glory.

And, in it all, *God is not finished.* God is just moving your life along to something greater. God took Elijah from beside that dry brook and led him to Zarephath where he began to feed a dying woman and her little son. Then God took him from there to Mt. Carmel where, in the greatest event in his life, he stood before all the forces of Baal, and Jezebel herself, and he called down fire from heaven and restored the worship of the true God to all of Israel and saved the nation.

So God is still in control. God is not helpless. When the brook dries up, God is in it. It is not a disaster to Him, although it may seem a disaster to you. He is saying, Move on now. I want to lead you to another step in your life. If you are obedient and open and loving, and let your faith be strengthened by Him, He will move you on up to new and greater things.

Would you come to move up, and move out, and move on? God loves you — He is leading — and He will lead you along. It does not make any difference where you are, or what you have done. The brook is dried up — the fight has gone out — you have sinned against Him — you have not loved Him like you ought to — but He loves you. He will forgive you and He will save you through Jesus Christ, the Lord and Savior of your life.

Commit yourself to Him — take your stand for Him — declare your faith.

BATTLING THE BLUES!

I Kings 19:1-10

Erma Bombeck has a little book entitled, *IF LIFE IS A BOWL OF CHERRIES, WHAT AM I DOING IN THE PITS?* Doesn't that express how we feel a lot of the time? Sometimes, you know, you go in to the desk and you start shuffling papers — you just cannot take hold of anything. You move it over here and over there — and then you do the little piddling things. You just cannot take hold of the big things that are facing you. You just push them aside and wait for the coffee break so you can walk out of the office and stand around and talk a little and get away from it. In the pits!

A woman gets up in the morning — just cannot get out of bed but she has to get the children off — they are gone — the house is empty and she has a day ahead and work to do. But she cannot get dressed — she sits at the table and drinks coffee and waits — then, she picks up the phone and calls two or three people. Finally, she just goes back to bed. In the pits! That is what we are talking about — Battling The Blues.

The National Institute of Health says depression is the number one psychological problem today! Eight million people in 1984 sought professional help or medical counseling for depression. They estimate that over 15 million others battled it through with some help — but did it on their own. They say there were 800 million prescriptions written that year by doctors in the United States — 25 percent of those were for mood altering drugs.

That simply says to you and to me that we are coping with a universal problem — a common problem. We even find many great people who were troubled with moods of depression. Abraham Lincoln was a prime example. He suffered great periods of depression. He was an introverted person to begin with and his biography reveals story after story when he would hit the bottom and was in the pits for a long time. But he kept on — he made it — he did great things. Even Sigmund Freud had his periods of depression. Martin Luther was given to depression. There were times when he did not even believe that God was alive. His wife confronted him, Is God dead? You are acting like He is.

So—I want to talk about depression. Not a one of us is immune to it — not even us preachers. We are just as ordinary and plain as anyone else. We have to deal with the same kind of problems. I heard of a fellow whose mother called to him, "Son, get up, it's Sunday morning: He just rolled over. She said 'Get up, you will be late for Sunday School. He opened one eye and said," I do not want to go to Sunday School' Well, give me one good reason why you shouldn't go to Sunday School. He said, I will give you two good reasons — number one, I don't like Sunday School; and number two, those people down at that church do not like me - they are all against me. With hands on her hips, she said, Son, I am going to give you two good reasons why you should go to Sunday School this morning — one, you are 35 years old; and number two, you are the pastor of the church! This is common to all of us. Battling the blues. We all have to face it.

This story in I Kings tells of a man who was really down in the pits. And it indicates to us that, basically, depression is a spiritual problem. It has its physical and psychological dimensions — but until we face it as a spiritual problem also, we really have not come to grips with it. We have more things today than any generation that has ever lived on the earth, yet we have more depression. You are not immune just because you are affluent. In fact, when you seem to be at your peak, suddenly you can get depressed. That indicates it is not material, it is not physical, it is not external; it is something internal— that intangible thing that we call spiritual.

Even the great spiritual men of the Bible had problems with depression. The Bible says David was a man after God's own heart. Yet David hit the bottom again and again. He found a way out because he found the spiritual solution. Jeremiah was called the weeping prophet because he wrote so many things clouded with the black ink of depression.

But here we have the story of Elijah, this great old prophet of God, of thunder and lightning, this daring brave man of the desert with his girdle of skin, a giant of a man with courage yet he whimpers and cries like a baby, in depression.

This story is a perfect pattern of the cause and treatment of depression. In Elijah's life, 2700 years ago, we find the soundest principles of psychology, the very prescription you would get from a psychologist or doctor today to battle depression. A man said to me, I went into deep depression a couple of years ago - what you said in the life of Elijah was exactly the ladder that I climbed to get back on top.

The story — Israel's king Ahab had married that idolatrous woman who worshiped Baal. She had brought with her 450 prophets of Baal and 400 prophets of Ashtoreth, the pagan gods of the Canaanites. And all the nation was being led away from God by this wicked woman Jezebel.

One day Elijah marched into the presence of the

33

king and the queen and said, By the authority of almighty God, judgment is coming upon you and your reign and your people. There shall not be one drop of rain from the heavens until you repent. For three and a half years there was drouth. The people were falling to their knees, the king was wringing his hands in desperation— he had a national crisis an his hands — no rain — no rain — no rain.

At last, he called Elijah for help. Tell me what God wants me to do. Elijah came. Have Jezebel bring all her 450 prophets of Baal and the 400 others to Mt. Caramel. We will have a contest and we will let the living God speak. The nation of Israel gathered to watch. Elijah simply said, If Baal be God, choose him; if Jehovah be God, choose him. Prepare an offering and call down your god to demonstrate his power.

The 450 prophets of Baal built the altar and offered the sacrifice. They prayed and shouted and sang and cut themselves all day long. Nothing happened. Toward evening Elijah built the altar and laid the sacrifice. Bring water and soak this offering until the wood is drenched and water stands in the ditches around the altar. And Elijah prayed. The heavens opened and fire came down and consumed that altar.

You can explain it many ways. It was supernatural. The finger of God reached down. Or, God created and made the world — in His hands this world moves even today — by His authority and power, He sent a bolt of lightning out of the sky. Anyway, the living God made His presence known. Fire came and, literally, the altar exploded and fire consumed it all. The people said, Jehovah is God! Elijah said, Take the prophets of Baal. They were slain and the religion was destroyed.

That is what happened to Elijah. What a great moment! A mountaintop experience! Nothing this great had ever happened in all his life. Then Jezebel hears about it over at Samaria, the capital. She says, Send a message to Elijah: May the gods strike me dead right now if by this time tomorrow I have not killed you! Pretty strong words — and it scared Elijah to death — it really got him down. What did he do?

From the mountaintop of victory, Elijah starts running as fast as he can to get out of there. He runs through that pass at Megiddo, across the plains of Sharon, down the trail that is a straight shot to the Negev. He reaches Beer-sheba and lets his servant stop; and he goes another day's journey into the wilderness. Finally, completely exhausted, he falls under a juniper tree. And he was in the pits. Lord, let me die, let me die. I have so many troubles. It is enough, Lord, take away my life.

I heard about the hod carrier, a fellow who carries brick on the job. It was hot in July and so hard and the bricks were so heavy. He said, Oh, Lord, this is so hard, I wish I were dead. About that time, a brick mason dropped a brick, and it hit his head and knocked him flat. "Lord, don't take me so seriously. I didn't really mean it." And Elijah did not really mean it. If he really wanted to be dead, Jezebel was just waiting to accommodate him. But he did not mean it; he was in the pits.

So — here we have the cause and the cure of depression. Right here. So simple — so direct — so sound. It is the ladder out of the pits, step by step. The same thing that happened to Elijah happens to us.

THE CAUSE

First, Elijah *lost his physical stamina.* He had run 300 miles, and another day's journey after that — without stopping, without eating, without resting. No wonder he was in the pits. He was physically exhausted. That is the first thing we observe in ourselves. We are

35

just exhausted.

Somebody said to me a long time ago: Do not ever make an important decision when you are tired and exhausted. Some of us do not take care of ourselves physically. We abuse our bodies. We get into the wrong habits of sleeping and eating. We are down physically. And, along with that, comes depression.

Second, *Elijah* was having a *natural reaction to a mood swing.* When you have a high, it is inevitably followed by a low. When you have been so high, sometimes you can drop so low so quickly.

Elijah had been at the greatest event in his life — the greatest experience — the greatest demonstration of the power of God he had ever seen. And he had been the center of it! The greatest victory in all his ministry. He had been at the peak. Psychologically, it is not unnatural or unusual for us to drop to a low after we have been so high. We have these swings. This is one of the psychological contributions to understanding ourselves today in saying there are these mood swings; and they do tend to follow such patterns.

It happens to a woman. Her daughter is getting married. Oh, the excitement! Months of preparing for the wedding — planning and buying the clothes — the dinners and celebrations — the parties. Then the wedding. Suddenly, her daughter is married and gone. After that high, she goes home and sinks to the low. The nest is empty — she cries — the baby girl is gone. That is natural.

It happens many times when a baby is born. There are nine months of physical concentration as the baby is on its way — the expectation and the buildup — the changing of life patterns. Then the baby is born — and the baby is home. Suddenly, you are into the routines of taking care of that baby — and depression comes three to six months after the baby is born. It is natural;

it is going to happen. Do not feel that something terrible is happening to you because you are in depression. As you swing down, you can swing up. It is not the end of the world.

A third cause: *He had lost his fellowship with other people.* He had withdrawn from other people and that brings on depression. There was a song — Everybody needs somebody. We all need each other. At college, the Baptist Student Union sponsored prayer partners. That was one of the greatest things for a student, away from home, lonely and frustrated. It may not sound very sophisticated today — but I want to tell you, it meant that somebody cared. We met and prayed together about each other's problems. We needed each other. When you withdraw and are by yourself and cut off from people, you go into depression.

Elijah now is sitting there under a juniper tree alone. He even goes farther into the Sinai — to Mt. Horeb where Moses received the Ten Commandments — and hides in a cave — as far away from the world as he can get — the worst thing he could do. He was in the pits.

Fourth, he had *withdrawn from God.* He had taken his eyes off God. Lord, I am the only one left — nobody else is true to you — I am the only one. Let me die, Lord. Take me out of it. I have spent my life working for you and we have built so much. Now, they have wiped it out. Jezebel is trying to kill me. She is going to kill everyone of the prophets of God. Only I am left.

You see, Elijah began to look around him at his problems, rather than looking to God. God is still on His throne. He still has that nation in His hands; and He still has your life in His hands. Elijah took his eyes off God and began to look at Jezebel: You can look at your critics — you can look at your enemies — you can look at those who say harsh things about you — those who threaten you — those who ridicule you — you can look at them and you will go into depression. You are looking at the wrong thing. Keep your eyes on God.

Those are some of the causes of depression. What did God do to bring Elijah out of the pits? God did three simple things:

THE CURE

God put Elijah to sleep. The angel woke him and he found food and water. He ate and went back to sleep. The angel woke him a second time after a long, long sleep and said, Eat, drink, for you have much ahead. You need strength.

The first thing we need to do is to get ourselves straightened out physically. Get back into routines and habits that will give us rest. Get to be the physically disciplined person you ought to be. That is the first step out of depression. Get disciplined — get hold of yourself — get hold of your habits — get hold of your activities — get hold of eating — get hold of your sleeping. Second, *God showed Elijah his sin.* You are sinning. Lord, how am I sinning? You are not trusting me — you are not believing in me — you are not believing I have a purpose — and that you are my man — you are not believing my hand is upon you — you are not believing I am using you. You are believing that Jezebel has taken this world and the prophets of Baal are on the throne. That is a sin to say, I do not believe in the power of God to work out His purpose in this world!

God said, Elijah, there are 7,000 others that have not bowed their knee. You are not the only one. I am still on the throne. You are sinning against me when you look on the dark side and become a pessimist saying, What's the use? I give up. You are sinning against me! He showed him his sin.

Third, *God put Elijah to work*. Go back, Elijah, get busy. Get to doing something. Instead of sitting around, wallowing in self-pity and feeling sorry for yourself, go back. You have a new king — you have to anoint Jehu as king. Ahab is dead — there is no king of Israel — and they need a king. Go back and anoint the new king.

Also, you are not going to live forever, Elijah. Go back and find a young man plowing in the field. His name is Elisha. Put your mantle on his shoulders. Teach him and train him and send him out to carry on the work. He sent him back to work. He sent him back to service. He sent him back to do something for somebody else and get the focus off himself.

I read just recently a statement about well-being. A person who has a sense of well-being has something bigger and larger in life than self; and has a bigger and larger purpose than self-service and self-fulfillment and self-satisfaction. When those people — regardless of where they are in life, financially or socially or in any other way — when they find themselves poured out in service to something bigger and larger than themselves, they inevitably have a sense of well-being, of purpose, of destiny, and a sense of approval of God on their lives. So — he pulls Elijah out of himself and says, Get turned outward now. Get to serving — get to work — get your eyes off yourself.

The question now is: *How are you going to handle your life?* First of all, *act now*. This is one of the problems of depression. You cannot make a decision. You keep putting off decisions. God said to Elijah, Get up and act now. Do something about it now.

Secondly, *move toward people*. Move away from yourself. All around you are people who need you — who need what you can do and give — who need your friendly hand — who need your kind word. Such little things. But, move toward people — forget about what

39

is wrong with you.

Third, *move toward service* — believing as the old-time preacher, Horace Bushnell, preached, Every life has a plan of God. Believe God put you here for a purpose. There is a plan for your life and you must fulfill that plan. Then, you are able to say, I am fulfilling it in the name of God. What I do is not for myself, it is for God.

Elijah had this sense of destiny and purpose — you and I ought to have it, too, because we are no different. God has a plan for every life. Move toward service.

And, *move toward God.* You cannot do it by yourself, none of us can. We will wallow and die in the pits without God. He puts a ladder before us and says, Move toward me. We can be directed and controlled in many directions. Some people are *inner-directed.* They are directed only by what satisfies them.

Some people are *outer-directed.* They are directed by the pressures put on them — whether it is criticism, circumstances or misfortune — whatever it is, they are directed by outer circumstances.

But the people who really make it great are those who are *upper-directed* — who look up and say, God, as best I know, I am giving myself in a commitment to you, I am going to do this for your glory. I am going to serve — I am going to pour out my life in service in your name. And, in so doing — being God-directed, upper-directed— you climb the ladder out of the pits.

THE MASTERY OF DISCOURAGEMENT

II Kings 13:14-19

There is a legend that the devil had an auction of all his tools to raise a little money. So he put his tools on display with a label on each tool giving the name and the price he would take for it. There was pride, and jealousy and greed, and lust — all the tools that the devil uses to get into the hearts of men and women.

But one strange-looking tool did not have a label on it or a price. Someone asked, How about that tool? He said, That is not for sale. How come — you are selling all the rest of them? Oh, I could not part with that tool — it is the only tool I need. If I have that tool, I can get into the heart and life of any person; and I can devastate a Christian with that tool. It is not for sale. What is the name of that strange-looking tool? And the devil said, That tool is *discouragement*. If I can just get a person discouraged to where they will give up and quit in discouragement, I will get them. It is better than any of the rest of these tools.

Discouragement. That is what I talk about — *the mastery of discouragement* — the devil's chief tool. Do you feel discouraged today? The nearest and dearest thing in life has gone from you; you are so lonely and the wound of sorrow and grief is so deep. You have tried to go on, but it is so hard. You are at the point now of saying, I am just so discouraged — I just don't think I can keep going on. Discouraged by loneliness. You have financial anxieties — setbacks. You have tried and tried and tried — yet, everything seems to go wrong and you are just ready to say, I quit — I am just ready to give up. Discouraged.

Shipwrecked marriage. Just cannot get it together. You have tried and you have tried and the spouse does not want to try, and so you are just discouraged — I will just quit even trying. Or moral failure. You have tried, again and again and again. But you are so discouraged — you just seem to fail anyway. That is what we talk about now.

I use this little incident from the story of one of the kings of Israel. And it is the story of the prophet Elisha, who took Elijah's place. Elisha has served through four kingdoms in Israel; now he is an old man — 80 years old — and he is sick unto death. The old king of Israel has died and the young son is on the throne. Joash is inexperienced, insecure, and frightened with the awesome responsibilities. To the north and the east, the enemy, Syria, amasses the armies on the border and prepares to march against Samaria the capital and against Israel the nation. They say, Now is our chance with this young king on the throne — he is not what his daddy was — we can take the kingdom.

Joash, terrified, comes to seek out the prophet of God, and finds him weak, broken, sick unto death. He is moved and so distressed that he falls across his body and, weeping over his face, he cries out, Oh, my father, my father. His daddy the king is dead — but— here — my father — my spiritual father. Then he says, The horsemen of Israel and the chariots thereof. What does he mean?

The horsemen of Israel. The chariots of Israel. You are the defense of our nation. But it is God who must defend us — and you are His prophet and you are dying. What are we going to do? Joash was wise enough to recognize that the defense of a people lies not in the armies on the front — the military or economic strength of a nation — the ultimate strength of a nation lies in godly men and women. The moral and spiritual depth of the people of God are the horsemen and chariots of America today. We need to remember that.

Elisha — ready to die — realizes that he still has a ministry to perform. He realizes that God has sent this boy king — and he has yet a message to give to him from God. So this strange symbolic ritual takes place.

I want you to see the power of it as God would speak through the prophet to you and to me today. We have cried and said, Oh what am I going to do? — oh, my father, my father — the horsemen and chariots thereof to protect my life — it has all gone to pieces — and I am so discouraged and frightened and worn out and afraid. Here is a message for you and me today. So, what does Elisha do?

The first step: *Submission*. Raising a trembling finger, Elisha points, Get your bow and an arrow. So the boy grabs his bow and arrow and brings them to Elisha. Elisha puts his hands upon the hands of the young king and blesses his hands, his talent, his weapons and his skill. I think he prays a prayer: Lord, take this young man's warrior skills and his skills to be a king and bless them and use them as he commits them to you.

That is the symbolism throughout the Old Testament. In the early chapters of Genesis we read: The prophet of God laid his hand upon the bow and the arrow and the hand of the warrior and blessed it. In the New Testament, in the ordination we lay on hands — we send people out, committing and consecrating them to God.

So this first act is a symbolism of submission to God and the blessing of God when we submit to Him — when we bring all that we have and lay it before Him

43

and let His hands rest upon us as we submit to Him.

That is the first step we must take — the step of submission — to bring not just our lives — what we are and who we are — but to bring our problems — our burdens — our difficulties — that which is overwhelming you, and you cannot handle — bring it before God and let His hands rest upon you — submitting yourself to Him.

And you can feel His touch. We read in the New Testament how many times Jesus reached out and touched people. He touched the blind man at the pool of Siloam — He touched his eyes and made him to see. The leper came to Capernaum — He touched him and he was made whole. The girl — He took her by the hand and lifted her up. The woman with the disease of blood touched Him — and He turned and said, Who touched me? He felt power going from Him to someone else. Someone touched me. Oh, the crowds are all around you — it could be anybody. No, there was someone who touched me and my power went into her life. The woman spoke, I did, Lord. He said, Be made whole.

You and I could have this experience at the hand of Christ, the loving Savior, touching you and me. It is a testimony to the witness of thousands again and again. I came in submission; I felt Him touch me and He changed me. That is the first step — submission.

The next step: *Action*. Elisha says, Open the window to the east. Opening the shuttered window, he looked — somewhere to the north and east, the armies of Syria were drawn up. It is interesting to note that Syria is a nation from antiquity; 3000 years ago Syria and Israel were fighting across the same boundaries that are there today. Elisha instructed the young king: Shoot the arrow into the air — eastward toward them. The second step is *action*. Take the initiative — do battle against the enemy.

Why is action the second step in overcoming discouragement and despondency and despair? It gets us out of inactivity. Psychologists tell us this is the soundest thing to do. Here, 800 years before Christ, is a master psychologist — a prophet of God — saying, Get up and get to acting it out. You change inside by acting outside. Act like you love; soon you will begin to love. Do loving acts and you find yourself loving inside.

We get it backwards. We say, How could I do something when I do not feel it inside? Do it, and you will get to feeling it. That is what Dr. Songer said in the Bible study of the Beatitudes. Act it out — then you get it inside. But we want to get it inside — when I have it here, then I will start acting. If I do not feel it, I do not do it. If I do not feel loving, I will not be loving. If I do not feel joy, I will not be joyful. Turn it around — act like you are joyful — act like you are happy — act it out — soon you will be changing inside. Act it out.

Those who deal with extreme situations of depression, grief and sorrow, say the worst thing to do is to stay by yourself, brooding, looking in on yourself. Get out — get going — see people — move out — do things — soon you forget about yourself. Even though you do not feel like doing it, you must do it! Act it out!

Commitment — submission. Then start doing something about it. One little arrow — an enemy you cannot even see — thousands and thousands of troops. That seems to be very ineffective. But it is like saying, I am going to begin to face the problem — I am going to tackle it and I am going to start now. I am going to do something. Regardless of how little and insignificant it is, I will get to working on it — I will get to doing. That is the step.

Now — the third step: *Faith*. As Joash shot that arrow, the prophet of God said, The arrows of the Lord's deliverance! Shoot it with *faith*. Remember,

45

God is on your side, and it is the arrow of the Lord's deliverance. It seems so little and insignificant. But with the power of God behind it — it is the Lord that will give you the victory. You do not win the battle against Syria with one little arrow shot by the king into the air. But when God comes in, He so multiplies that arrow — He so gives it His power that it will be the victory over Syria. When you acknowledge that God is on your side, God is with you and God is going to see you through. That is faith! Believing even though it seems impossible, I do it in the name of God and God will see me through — He will give me victory!

David was just a little shepherd-boy when he faced Goliath. Goliath, leader of the Philistine armies, was almost twice as tall as David. He had a spear that was ten feet long. He weighed twice as much as David weighed. He had stymied the armies of Saul for 40 days and nights in the Valley of Elah. The Philistines were drawn up on one side and the forces of Saul on the other, and no one dared to go down and fight against this giant.

And here came David — dressed in a shepherd's toga and sandals — a staff in his hand and a slingshot at his side. Goliath just roared in laughter and ridicule when he saw David and said, Am l a dog that you send a boy with a stick to run me off? I will cut off your head and feed it to the ravens. Get out of here, boy. You have not lost any sheep down here.

But David picked up five small stones from the brook, balanced them in his hand, picked one and put it in his slingshot. He wound up and let it go. As it went, he said, The battle is the Lord's! Not the battle is David's — the battle is Israel's —the battle is Saul's. The battle is the Lord's! The stone went straight to Goliath and hit him in the forehead and he fell to the ground. With Goliath's sword, David cut off his head and dispersed the armies of Philistia and Israel was saved.

The arrow of the Lord's deliverance! The stone that says, The battle is the Lord's! The little effort that you and I make — and how little it is — does not make any difference. If God is with us He says He will see us through.

So — you have *submission* first; and then you have *action*; and you have faith. And, then . . . .

The fourth ingredient: *Persistence*. As the king stood by the window, Elisha said, Boy, get that quiver of arrows. He got the quiver. Take that quiver of arrows and smite the floor! Hit the floor with all your arrows now. The boy slammed them on the floor. The prophet said, Good, good. The boy slammed them again and the prophet said, Good. He hit it a third time — Good. And the boy laid down the quiver, so proud of himself, and came to the prophet.

He had won his approval. What does that mean, sir?

But the prophet was angry. Son, why did you quit? I thought three times was enough. No. You must keep on and on and on. If you had struck the floor seven times, eight times — if you had beaten that floor until you beat the ends off the arrows — God would have given you endless victory. Because you quit, you will only defeat Syria three times. After that, you will be defeated —because you will not stay with it. God put his finger on the flaw in this boy's character. If you are going to quit you will never be victorious.

So — the fourth ingredient — *Persistence*. I will keep on keeping on. And that is the hard thing in life. You see, God has taken a big paintbrush and painted this area where you are right now — He has painted it yellow and said, No Parking Here, to every one of us.

47

We cannot park and stay put in life. We have to keep moving — we have to keep going on. Any time we pull out and park God says, You are going to lose some of the victory I want to give you. You are going to miss it — unless you keep on keeping on. That is hard to do, especially when things are not going right for us and every step seems a little harder. But keep on keeping on — keep smiting the floor with the arrows — and God will give you the victory.

Our country was settled by people who came over those Alleghenies in ox wagons. They followed those wagons through the forests — over the mountains — through the passes — through the snow and the desert — all the way to the California coast to settle a nation. I have seen oxen all over the world. They are the slowest plodding creatures I have ever seen. Hitched to a plow or a wagon, they just plod along. I can imagine those early settlers as they followed those ox wagon caravans — they made little progress — just slowly plodding along. At night they would circle and feed the stock and get up the next day and plod along with the ox wagons another day.

That is the way of life — life is an ox wagon existence for most of us. We go so slowly, but we have to keep at it — keep at it. And we have to keep the direction upward and onward — westward. It is not like a race at Churchill Downs with the shouting and excitement and it is over within two minutes. It is a long time ox pull. Keep on keeping on.

The great lessons of life are all around us. Ernest Hemingway wrote a score of stories and received rejection after rejection before he ever had a story published. But he kept on and on and on to become a great writer. Look at the great basketball players. They miss more shots than they make. Hank Aaron missed more balls than he hit, but he kept on swinging

48

and he kept on shooting and he kept on going. Life around us is full of examples of those who said, I will not quit — I will not be discouraged — I am going to keep going on because I am committed to God — I know He is with me. His hand is upon me — I know it is by His power that I will do it. I have faith in Him. I am just going to keep on going and let Him give me the results. I will be faithful — I will be persistent. We all face discouragement, even a preacher. You think because we preach a sermon about discouragement and mastering it that we are masters and overcome discouragement. We are no different than you are. I often say, I put my britches on just like any other man. I am just as human as any person. I struggle. And every preacher struggles against discouragement.

I want to tell you of one of the greatest preachers in the United States today — Dr. Norman Vincent Peale. You would not think he would ever be discouraged, but here is the story from his own personal experience. I have been with him and I know him personally and I always see this exuberant, enthusiastic person who generates such confidence and gives it to so many people.

Dr. Peale was pastor of the Marble Collegiate Church when his book, *THE POWER OF POSITIVE THINKING*, came out. When it hit the best seller list, every preacher and theologian in the country took him to task. He became popular, and there was jealousy. They could not see someone getting this kind of prominence. They began to pick his theology to pieces. He is nothing but a charlatan. He is just palming off psychology for religion — he has no gospel in his preaching, and they pointed out the weaknesses. They coined snide phrases about him. Pealeism — that is Pealeism, that is not the gospel of Jesus Christ — he is not a Biblical preacher. I heard one speaker say, Paul is appealing, but Peale is appalling. He became so discouraged and disillusioned when even his brethren in the ministry and the theologians in his own seminary began to attack him. He said, I was ready to quit preaching, and I wrote out my resignation. Then the death of his father delayed his making a decision.

His stepmother came to see him shortly after the funeral and he told her what he was going to do. She bristled up and said, Norman, let me tell you what your father said just before he died: Don't let that boy be upset by those jackasses — that is the word she used — in the ivory towers of the seminary and in their pulpits — they are jealous of him. I have heard him preach — I know he believes the gospel — I know he preaches the gospel. He is just putting it down where everybody can understand it — he is doing it to help people — he must keep on preaching. She shook her finger in his face and said, Young man, don't you do that now. You get back to preaching. And he tore up his resignation and went on preaching.

Discouraged. We all need these simple steps — we need to say, I am *committed* to God — all that I am belongs to Him — I have *submitted* myself to Him. I will act — I will not sit here feeling sorry for myself — I am going to do something — I am going to help people in the name of Christ. I am going to have *faith* — the arrow of the Lord's deliverance. And then I am going to stay with it, Lord. I will *persist* to the very end. And God will give you the victory!

You were on a low limb this morning. Let's climb to a high limb today. Make a commitment to Christ anew and afresh today.

Whatever it is you need to do, do it today.

TURNING ADVERSITIES
INTO VICTORIES
II Chronicles 32:1-8

Our community has been shocked and stunned by the tragic murder of two fine young high school students. Many, many questions have come about how God could let something like this happen to any of us. Where is God that such a crime can happen to apparently such innocent victims? Of course, this is the larger question of life about adversities, heartbreaks, disappointments, and tragedies that happen. And we grope for the answer to the question, Why? There is often not an answer. We cannot logically put together a reasonable process that says, This is why that happened to this person or to me.

But we do come to another question. Even though we cannot answer the question of why we must recognize the fact of adversity and tragedy. And the real question is, How do I react and respond to it? How can I cope with it and deal with it? Even if we could answer the question, why, it would not make any difference if we could not answer the second question, How can I cope with it? That is what is really important. It is said many times, the same sun softens butter and hardens clay. And the same adversity in life will enable some people to advance over adversity and be victorious; and other people will be hardened and defeated and go down to destruction.

So — what I talk about is, literally, *ADVANCING*

OVER OUR ADVERSITIES. We have a wonderful story and example in the scripture. Let's get the setting and the background.

It is the 8th century before Christ in the little kingdom of Judah. II Chronicles 32:1 starts this way: After these things, then came Sennacherib! Strange words. What is involved in that verse? After *what* things? We discover what things in the previous chapter. After the great religious reforms of the good, righteous young king Hezekiah, then came Sennacherib. Hezekiah had come to the throne as the son of Ahaz. And Ahaz, we read, was one of the wickedest kings that Judah ever had. He was weak — he yielded to every temptation — he brought idolatry and paganism to Judah. The people followed him and went down, down, morally and spiritually into idolatry. Then came this young son, Hezekiah, to the throne. And Hezekiah, in contrast to his father as the worst king in all of Judah, becomes one of the best kings Judah ever had.

He comes to the throne at age 25. He is godly — he is righteous — he is spiritually sensitive — he is an attractive young leader — he is a reformer. He opens the temple and cleanses it and brings it back into use. He destroys the pagan altars throughout the land and burns the idols. He reestablishes the observance of the Passover among the Jews. He restores true religion and the word of God became the word of the people and the priests taught it. He institutes justice, morality, mercy and decency. The nation had this great religious revival. For a whole decade, they honored God and served Him and lived like God wanted them to live. And, after these things, then came Sennacherib.

Get the force of it! Get the power of it! Get the big question mark in the hearts of all the people! O God, we are your children! This is your nation! We honor you — we live for you. Now, after all these things, here comes

Sennacherib.

Sennacherib is the king from the southeast at Nineveh — the king of Assyria. He comes marching with his hordes of soldiers and chariots to conquer the civilized world — taking captives by the thousands — murdering women and babies — burning cities and crops and scorching the land. He sweeps northwest through Syria and present day Turkey as far as Tarsus and down to the Greek isles. He mounts a flotilla, takes some of the Mediterranean Islands and lands on the coast of present day Lebanon. He marches victoriously through the Dog River pass, that famous pass through which the conquerors of history have come — across the Leontes River between Tyre and Sidon and into the land of the Philistines and Israelites. Then he turns inward to the walled city of Lachish, just beyond the borders of Jerusalem, puts it under siege, and watches that city slowly die of starvation. From his royal tent, he sends word to Hezekiah: We are coming against you — we are going to do the same thing to Jerusalem; and we are going to take all your people captive.

See this red horde — dressed in their scarlet tunics, with their red shields, their chariots and their horses, sweeping through the land. The very anti-God himself. He belittles and ridicules the people of Judah. He scorns their God and makes fun of him. Call on your God and he will fall before me like all the gods of the other cities.

So — he profanes God and he attacks God's people — he now has Lachish under siege. And the people say, O God, how can you let this happen to us? Then came Sennacherib! The people, perplexed and confused, said, Where is God? Why doesn't God do something? See their cries leaping up from the pages of this book. We have done our best. I have tithed and I have gone to church and I have been faithful. We are a decent moral family and we are good Christian people — our children are in church every Sunday. And now, here comes Sennacherib! Here comes adversity. Tragedy! Sorrow — murders — deaths — sickness — here it comes! O Lord, why?

It is not unique. We see this story played out all through the scriptures. That was what Job said. Job was the finest man of his day — godly, moral, decent, literally the child of God in a wicked world. But he lost it all. The Chaldeans carried his children into captivity. They stole his flocks and his livestock. He lost his friends — he lost his reputation — he even lost his health. We find him a pauper sitting on the ash heap outside the city with his body covered with sores. He is crying, O God, why? Why? If you are God and I am yours, why does this happen to me?

From Abraham to Paul all the way through this book, there is the cry. Paul could have said again and again, Why, Lord? Beaten, jailed, left for dead, finally martyred. Why, O Lord? John — the faithful disciple of God is on Patmos in exile saying, Why? Why me, O Lord?

That is the universal question that is asked even today. One of the grandest missionaries I have known is Hal Boone in East Africa. How effective he was. How powerful he was in his work in Kenya. One night, driving that road from Nairobi to Mombasa, he let his 16-year-old son take the wheel while he slept in the back seat. They had a terrible accident. The son was not injured. Hal Boone's back was broken. He was paralyzed from his hips down confined to a wheelchair for the rest of his days. Now, back from the mission field — he is at home in Texas. Again and again, Oh, God, why this choice servant of yours? Then came Sennacherib into his life! You have asked it and I have asked it.

But, I say again, we do not have the answer to why. Paul says, We know that all things work together for the good of them that love God. Somehow God can take all the bad things in life and, with His children in His hand, He can work them together. So we do not find the answer to why, now. Someday we may. One day we will see it from the beginning to the end, and we will understand. Furthermore, in asking the question, why did God do this, we need to say, God did not do it. It is operating within His permissive will — but do not blame God for it. Do not say that God is helpless in it.

A lot of things happen to us over which God would say, I have nothing to do with bringing that upon you. Physical circumstances, the laws of nature. You jump off this building and you cannot say God made you splatter on the pavement. God did not make it happen. You chose to do it, and it is the law of gravity that overcame you and pulled you down. Your choice did it. But we do not say, God did these things. We say, Within the permissive will of God, old Sennacherib comes.

Evil is loose in the world and the devil has his way now, and our answer to that is the question, How do we handle it? What do we do with it? And we look again to Hezekiah. How did he handle this adversity? How did he deal with Sennacherib?

Adversities can become advancements for us. We can convert them from defeats into victories when we do as Hezekiah and the people of Judah did. What happened first? These adversities made them *look* up to God. Hezekiah spake to the people saying, Don't look down, don't look at these red-suited soldiers and their crimson shields and their fierce swords and spears and their terrifying chariots and horsemen. Don't look there.

Look up! Be strong and courageous, be not afraid nor dismayed for this king of Assyria, nor the multitude with him: for there be more with us than with him. With him is an arm of flesh; but with us is the Lord our God to help us and to fight these battles.

We have to come to this place in life, ultimately, all

55

of us to say, I cannot handle my life by myself — the arm of flesh is weak. When I depend upon the arm of flesh in my life, I will not make it. Regardless of whether it is sunshine or rain, I cannot handle success with the arm of flesh. I certainly cannot handle failure with the arm of flesh. I cannot handle decency and morality — I get so self-righteous and proud of myself and secure in myself with the arm of flesh. I cannot handle unrighteousness and sin and temptation with the arm of flesh.

Our tendency is to look at our resources, our capacities, our abilities and say, I can do it. That always leads to destruction.

We are never delivered from that self-made destruction until we look up and say, My life needs to be linked to the arm of God — God in my life and His power in me. I can do nothing of myself; I must have Him with me. The alcoholic will not make it as long as he says, I can handle it. He has to get to the very bottom when he says, I cannot handle it. The arm of flesh will not hold me up. I have to find the power greater than myself, outside myself, beyond myself, and ask that power to come in. It is the power of God. So — the first step is to look up.

A husband and wife said, We need help. That is the first step. Our marriage is on the rocks — we do not want it — neither of us — for our sakes, for our little child's sake. What can God do to help us? I could tell you that story, attaching different circumstances to it, again and again out of my life as a minister. When you get to the end of your rope — we cannot handle this marriage — this problem — this conflict — this personal temptation — tell me how God can come into my heart and life, into our marriage and home. That is the first step. Look up — and see an arm so strong that it never fails. The first step. God is with me.

The second step. Hezekiah said, *Rise up and act on*

your faith. You have expressed your faith in God — now let's get busy. He then took counsel with his mighty men. Plug the fountain of Siloam and the fountain that spills into the valley and cut off the water so when Sennacherib comes, his people will not have water to drink. Then build up the walls that have tumbled down. And they raised towers on the walls and made a second wall outside this old wall they had rebuilt. They built Millo, that high tower at the northeast corner of the city; and they made darts and shields in abundance.

Hezekiah organized his resources — rebuilding and fortifying with weapons and armament. He set captains over the people so everybody had a task in the defense force. Everybody knew what they were to do. Everybody was responsible to somebody else up the line, and they could be a unit marching together.

Our greatest achievements often come when we are under the pressure and stress of adversity. When we are drifting, just coasting — when nothing is demanded of us from life — when the pressure is not on us — we do not produce. But let the pressure of stress and adversity come, and we mobilize all the resources within us to achieve our best. It is a proven physiological and psychological fact as well as a spiritual fact that we advance greater and more forcefully under stress.

Here are some physical examples. Charles Rogers, a teenager in Tampa, Florida, was working on his automobile. He jacked it up and crawled under the differential, then the jack slipped from under the car and the car fell on him, pinning him and crushing his chest. He screamed for help. His mother and father came running and saw this 3500-pound car resting on their son. The father wisely knew he could not do anything about getting that car off the boy without a jack. He began to run, looking for a way to put it back.

But his little wife, Maxine, just 39 years old,

weighing 135 pounds and had been sick — got hold of the rear bumper and lifted up one corner of that car and her boy rolled free. Later on they tried, but neither the man himself, nor the man and boy together, could lift the corner of that car. But she did under stress.

Dr. Hans Selye at Montreal University, doing studies on stress, calls them stress miracles and they are all the same pattern. A 200-pound live bomb fell onto the deck of an aircraft carrier. This young sailor, seeing it was going to explode, picked it up singlehandedly and carried it to the side and threw it overboard.

Later, no one could even get their arms around it, much less lift 200 pounds and carry it! Yet, he did it under stress.

That is the simple principle — the whole body reacts to pump energy into our muscles. It is true spiritually, when God's power is in us. We can say as Paul says, I can do all things through Christ who strengtheneth me. When we look up — we can rise up able to do. Advancing through adversity, we never know how strong we are or what we can do. We never know how until we give God a chance to give us the power to go against the adversities of life and be victorious in them.

Adversities let us *hold up an example and testimony for God*. That is what happened next. God came. In a miraculous way, something swept through the enemy troops and 185,000 of them died. And Sennacherib returned with shame on his face to his own land — defeated. And many brought gifts unto the Lord to Jerusalem and Hezekiah was magnified in the sight of all the nations from henceforth. That is the means whereby God is magnified and glorified. He comes into our lives and we have these miraculous victories over adversities. People will say: How did you cope with it? How can you be so happy when these things have happened to you? How can you keep going? And you say, The Lord did it. If you let Him come into your heart and life, He can do it for you.

Let me tell you of Harry Hanners who advanced through adversity. He had always dreamed of teaching school. His wife, a nurse said, All right, Harry, you go back to school — I will work overtime to keep our family together and to pay your tuition so you can get equipped to get a job teaching school. So, over many adversities, sacrifices, and hardships he got his degree and got a job teaching school.

Harry was in seventh heaven. The family was active in church he was teaching a Sunday School class and leading a Boy Scout troup. Then one day he got a catch in his back and could not straighten up. The doctor said, You have TB of the spine — your spinal column is disintegrating. Thus came Sennacherib into the life of this wonderful family.

Surgery did not help. Seven operations over a period of three years. Sennacherib came again and again. But they kept their faith. He taught school in between the bouts in the hospital.

During this time, Harry took a lot of drugs to ease the pain and found he was addicted — going from one drugstore to another and one doctor to another — his life was going to pieces. Sennacherib kept zeroing in on him.

One day his wife said, Harry, I know you are addicted — you deny it but I know what you are doing. If you do not let God help you break this habit, I am going to leave you and you are going to wreck your life. Weeping, he pulled out a bunch of prescriptions, tore them up and flushed them down the toilet. They knelt there and said, Gone, gone, gone are my drugs. Harry committed himself to God anew and afresh and asked God to help him. His wife stayed with him through these terrible periods of withdrawal. They marked the calendar each day and he

59

fought the battle and overcame it. Three months later he was free of all addiction. Then came Sennacherib.

Two detectives came to the school and waited for him. We have been running down these prescriptions — we are arresting you as an addict and falsely securing narcotics. Sennacherib again. Harry pleaded guilty — what could he say — even though he was off drugs now, it did not make any difference.

In prison, however, he saw teenagers all around him with the same problems. He said to the warden, I am a schoolteacher — can I start a class and teach these boys? So Harry Hanners started a school in prison, resulting in the following statistics:

Four of these students took the high school equivalency test and passed it. Seven of them went on to college. One of them who was incorrigible had his life so transformed that he went out of prison and started a business and became a good citizen.

When Harry's service was over, the parole board said, We have been watching your work — we think we need a school like this in prison for teenagers. And Harry Hanners started the first program of that kind in the Nassau County jail.

When it was all over, I want you to hear what his wife said: When Harry was first convicted, our minister said, God must have a reason for letting him be put in jail. It was hard to believe then, but now we know that he was right. Harry has a career that is much more important and much more rewarding to him as a person and to us as a family, than anything else he could have done.

You see — he advanced over adversities because he let God into his life and heart so he could win the battle.

Will you do that? Will you put your hand in the nail-scarred hand of Jesus and let Him give you advancement over adversities in life?

WHEN TROUBLE COMES!

Psalm 23

A chauffeur in a great big black car was sailing down the expressway at 75 miles an hour. A trooper pulled him over, got out, leaned into the window and said, Let me see your driver's license — you were going 70 miles an hour and more! He said, Yessir, I know.

I have a good mind to give you a ticket. That's all right — give me two or three. Oh, you are a smart alec, huh? Well. I'm just a good mind to take you before the judge right now. Take me before two judges — I don't care. The trooper said, Come on, follow me.

They came to the little town. They came before the judge; the trooper told the judge what happened. The judge said, I think I'd better fine you $75 and costs right now. That's all right, make it $150. I don't care. Well, I'll give you six months in jail, too! Give me a year — it doesn't make any difference.

The judge said, What's the matter with you — are you crazy — who are you anyway? Well, I happen to be the chauffeur for the warden of the penitentiary! I'm in for life for murder and you can't do a thing to me! You can't touch me.

This morning — I want to talk about achieving a place in life where we can live above trouble — where trouble really cannot touch us — living beyond trouble. That is what this 23rd Psalm is all about — in the fourth verse where David says, "I will fear no evil: for thou art with me....

Now, let's get the full impact of that: The Lord is my shepherd— I will fear no evil: for thou art with me — Troubles — troubles — troubles — toils and tears — that is life, isn't it. But, when we become a Christian, it does not mean that God is going to build a wall around us, and we will never have any more troubles in life. No, not so.

Our Christian faith is not some kind of an imaginary fantasy — where we float off into some kind of unreal world, and do not even face the troubles of this life. Christianity is not like some kind of happiness pill — we can take the gospel and we are just happy from then on and never have to face a problem or trouble. It is not like an escapism that comes from the bottle where you can drink and your troubles are forgotten and you escape them for a little while. No!

Our Christian faith deals at the very level of reality always. There are troubles — troubles will come — disasters will happen. They will happen to all of us — even to you and to me as Christians.

You remember the earthquake in San Francisco— #4 on the Richter scale they said — and people are predicting that all of California is going to slide into the sea because it sits right on that fault.

And you may remember the terrible disaster in San Francisco many years ago which just leveled the city. But the strange thing — it left the Red Light district and the bars standing. Some newspaperman wrote these words: If, as they say, God spanked this city for being over frisky, why did he burn down all the churches and spare old Hopalong's whiskey?

We ask this question: Why do the righteous suffer and the unrighteous prosper? We should not hold out the false premise to people and say, This is our Christian theology — become a Christian and you will never have any kind of problem. Righteousness will always be rewarded, and unrighteousness always punished. Not so — not so!

Christian faith is not an escape from trouble. David says Christian faith gives us something with which to handle our troubles — a power — a resource — I will fear no evil — no trouble — because thou art with me.

Now — there are two points, two premises that I want us to lay hold on in this wonderful promise. First is this:

OUR TROUBLES ARE MANAGEABLE

With the help and power of God, we can manage our troubles. They are manageable. The Apostle Paul learned this. No man faced more troubles perhaps, in the Christian life, than the Apostle Paul.

In II Corinthians 4:8-9 Paul talks about their condition as Christians — his condition as a Christian — imprisoned, suffering, hardships of all kinds: We are troubled on every side, yet not distressed; we are perplexed, but not in despair. Persecuted, but not forsaken; cast down, but not destroyed.

Paul was simply declaring the faith that this shepherd boy had also. Though troubles come, I have the power and the resource to handle those troubles, because thou art with me.

I like the story I read of Dr. Leslie Weatherhead who was pastor of the great City Temple Church in London during the dark days of World War II when Hitler's buzz bombs were coming over and wreaking such destruction. So many thousands of people being killed.

One of his parishioners was asked whether she was afraid — how she was able to sleep during the buzz

63

bombs. She said, Why, they don't bother me! Our pastor says our Lord never slumbers nor sleeps. So I decided there was no need of two of us staying awake and worrying about it. Every night I just say my prayers and when I finish, I tell Hitler where to go. Then I lay my head on my pillow and go to sleep.

That is Christian faith. Tell the devil where to go, because your faith is in the Lord. I can go to sleep because his eye never sleeps. He is watching over us. That is what David was saying. Isn't that a great, glorious, wonderful promise!

I am sure that you, as I, studied the great writer of English prose and poetry — the favorite of all, I think, was Robert Louis Stevenson. He was a great writer — one of spiritual depth and truth — one who had moral values and quality in his stories. He became the acclaimed man of English letters. He toured the continent, lived in Paris, and received the accolades of all the great of that day. He came to the United States, made a whirlwind tour here, and married an American woman.

But then, you remember, sickness overtook him — tuberculosis. In those days they were unable to treat him, so he just lived in the grip of this disease that slowly consumed him. He finally went to the South Sea islands to find some relief in that climate. When Mrs. Dehoney and I went to a Baptist World Alliance meeting in Australia — we went to Tahiti. There I saw the little house where he lived. As I saw that house, the memorabilia scattered around — the chair, the desk, letters and other things — I thought about this man and his last days.

And his last days were his greatest. There was maturity, depth, quality in his writing. But, you know, those last days were struggles — by the hour he struggled. Wracked with pain, with despair, and physical exhaustion — he would rise up from the bed — he would get into the chair — he would compel himself to write for an hour — then, exhausted, he would go back to bed — all the time coughing up blood.

I remembered what he said in talking about his faith in God. Any man can see it through to midnight. In other words, you can always hold out to midnight. You can always hold out with the help of God — then it is another day — always hold out to midnight.

That is the promise. The Lord *is* my shepherd. He is with us today. He is not a Lord that is just going to come back in the second coming sometime out yonder. He is not a Lord that died on the cross 2,000 years ago for our sins. *He is my shepherd right now!* He can see me through the day. And, if that is so, I can make it! I can always make it to midnight.

David knew this. The reason he had such a faith — the Lord had seen him through this experience — and this experience — and this experience. Then David could say, As He saw me through this one — He will see me through the next one tomorrow, and tomorrow's tomorrow. He knew this even as a shepherd boy.

You remember, the armies of Philistia came against the Israelites in the valley of Elah. The Philistines were coming from the plains and the Israelites under King Saul were on the hilltops here. The Philistines challenged, Let's prove whether your God is the true God, or the gods of the Philistines are the true gods.

Goliath, their leader, challenged them. He cursed them in the name of Jehovah and profaned God's name for 40 days and 40 nights, saying, Come down and fight me — one man against me — and whoever shall win — that army will be victorious. And no one would go out — not even King Saul. Though he stood head and shoulders above other men, he dared not fight this giant Goliath.

65

Then there was a little teenage shepherd boy by the name of David who came into camp bringing some cheeses and some cakes to his older brothers who were in service to Saul. When he saw this going on he said, Why don't you fight Goliath? That giant? — we don't dare. David said, Seeing how he has defiled the name of the living God, you ought to go. I would fight him.

As you know, they brought David into the presence of Saul who said, We do not have any other volunteers; we will send you. Put my armor on, take my shield and sword. David replied, It is too big for me. I will just go as I have always done — with my shepherd's crook and my slingshot and my little sword here. I will face him and I will defeat him. They laughed at him.

David said, I know that the Lord will be with me. One night a bear came out against the flock and I went out and slew the bear. Another time a lion came, and I went out and, with my slingshot, I slew the lion. So I know the Lord that delivered me from the paw of the bear and the paw of the lion will also deliver me from the hand of this unrighteous giant.

You see, it is simple faith already manifest early in life. David said, The Lord was with me then — He was with me then. So I don't fear for tomorrow, the next step in life — because the same Lord that was there when I needed Him — He will be with me when I need Him tomorrow as I face the giant. That is how to live above trouble.

And, cannot everyone of us look back and say, Well, I did not know how I would get through — but the Lord saw me through. We can take the hand of a loved one and say we have had some rough times, but, you know, the Lord stood by us. He stood by us then — and then, remember — so why should I panic — why should I go to pieces when trouble comes now!

The Lord *is* — He exists *now* — He *is* present with

me — He *is my shepherd today*. Therefore, I will fear no evil. Thou art with me — you are standing at my side — you have been there before — you will be with me now — you will be with me tomorrow.

That is the first point here. Our troubles are manageable — if we really have this kind of personal faith in God through Jesus Christ to believe. He is real — He is present — He is personal. Jesus is mine, and I am His in a personal commitment and a personal faith.

Then, the second premise. . .

TROUBLE CANNOT REACH

THE REAL "ME"

I think this has another shade of meaning; let's catch it. I will fear no evil, for thou art with me — because trouble cannot reach the real me, anyway. The real me. Like that chauffeur, we get into a position where we can say to trouble — you can't touch me — I am out of your jurisdiction. There is a part of my life where not a thing in the world can happen that can really touch the thing that makes *me* what I am, and makes you what you are. Let me show you.

Let's use this illustration. If you go to the bank and want to borrow some money, they will say, Give us a financial statement. Put down all you possess — your assets over here. Then put down your debts over here. Let's balance them out and see what you are worth.

Instead of putting down the real estates you own, and the stocks you own and the money you have in the bank — those assets — let's put down our *personal assets* — the things that make us what we are. Get a ledger and write down what you really possess. You will discover these things cannot be touched by trouble.

67

For example, I would put down, first of all, *character* and *integrity*. Come what may in life, nothing can rob you of your character and integrity. Trouble cannot touch that.

Put down your *ability* — the mind and ability that God has given you. One of the inspiring stories of the depression years when I was a boy was the story of the man who started the Piggly-Wiggly stores. He went broke two or three times, but every time he hit the bottom during those dark days, there would come a story saying, I am not through. Though I lost my money — I lost my stores — I lost my business — I still have the *ability* to do it! I am keener than I have ever been and I will come back. Trouble cannot take your capacities and abilities away from you.

The third thing I would put down is *experience*. A man said to me the other day, I have been through a lot of trouble but, you know, I'm a lot smarter now than I was before I had the trouble. I learned something. Because I learned something, I am better off. Make all your troubles — instead of stumbling stones to defeat — stepping stones to greater success. Trouble cannot touch the experiences you have.

Trouble cannot touch the *relationships of love*. People who love you, and you love them — and your love for God, and God's love for you — trouble cannot touch that.

Finally, trouble cannot touch the *security* you have in Jesus Christ. Not a thing in this world that can happen can take Jesus Christ away from you — take His presence, His power — nothing!

So you see, the second point is: Actually, trouble does not have any jurisdiction over the real you and the real me. We do not need to fear evil, because evil just cannot even get to us. At the points where we really count, the Lord is with us.

68

There is a beautiful story I want to close with. I first heard this story from Angel Martinez, an evangelist and my classmate at the seminary. But I discovered the story is much older; I have read it in books that are over a hundred years old. It seems an English preacher told it a century-and-a-half or two centuries ago. An old-time story that illustrates what I am talking about.

It is a story about Jamie, the little shepherd boy. Jamie was dying — just an ignorant, illiterate under-privileged shepherd boy of the countryside — the mother, a widow, and very poor. The minister came to see Jamie as he was dying and tried to talk to him about life eternal, about security in God, about faith. Jamie was hardly old enough to understand, and certainly he was not educated enough to learn it all.

So the minister then said, I want to teach you something. You are a shepherd boy, Jamie, and I want to tell you about the good shepherd, the great shepherd who will look after you in the days ahead as you get ready to die.

His name is Jesus. And I want you to know Jesus as your shepherd. I want to teach you this Bible verse for you to recite: The Lord is my shepherd. The *Lord* is my shepherd.

Jamie could not quite learn it until the preacher said Do it this way. Let a finger stand for each word. *The* — *Lord* — is — my — shepherd. And Jamie learned that verse and recited it.

A few days later the mother came to the minister and said Jamie is dead. Would you come and have a funeral — say some words over him? The minister said, I will.

Then she said, It was strange when he died. His hands were in a strange position. When he died, we found this hand firmly grasping that finger. What do you reckon that meant?

The minister said, I know — as the time came and he knew he was dying, he was saying the verse I taught him. He was holding on to the most important part of that verse, The Lord is mine — my shepherd — I have claimed Him — and He has come to me.

Dear lady, I think the good shepherd came to take Jamie by the hand and lead him on across the river into the promised land. He was holding on to that promise in that moment.

Oh, that is the most important word in the English language for you and for me right now. My — is He mine — have you claimed Him? Do you know Him? Are you certain that Jesus Christ is your shepherd?

If not, I would not move without making my commitment to Him. He wants to lift you above the troubles of life and give you victory over them, here and hereafter.

IF YOU SUFFER LOSS

Psalm 42:1-5

After the long sleepless nights at the hospital you are finally standing by that bed. The nurse is holding the wrist of one you love dearly. She lays the hand on the sheet, looks up and says, There is no pulse. Your mother is gone. Suddenly, a wave of grief sweeps over you; you gasp for air as though stifled — and the hard reality comes that death has touched you for the first time.

Or, a young man paces the hospital hall; in the delivery room is that wonderful young wife of yours. You are so excited at the promise of new life. Then, the doctor comes and says, It is all over — you have a fine boy. Then his face grows long, But — your wife is not doing well — in fact, we have lost her. Suddenly, you cry out, Oh, God, no — it can't be.

Or, in the kitchen, you carelessly leave that pan of hot water on the stove with the handle out. The child, hardly more than two years old, reaches and pulls it down — scalding itself. Finally the child dies. You and your husband say, Oh, why does this happen — to an innocent one, too? It is all my fault — my carelessness.

Or a young seminary student has a fatal automobile accident. His father says to a friend at the seminary, I don't understand. Where was God when my son was killed? He was going to be a preacher and God let this happen to him!

Or, it does not have to be death for us to suffer loss. We can suffer the loss of something precious and dear to us and still have the same kind of grief, agony and pain. A husband says to his wife of many years, I'm through — I'm leaving you for this younger woman. And he does. There is divorce and the death of a marriage. Sometimes physical death is easier to accept than that kind of living death because you live in the hope that maybe it can be recaptured. But there is the same grief and sorrow.

Or it can be sorrow and grief at the loss of health or position. Phyllis Knight, well known by the Louisville community as a broadcaster and reporter at WHAS, went through this terrible experience of mental depression and collapse. She has shared publicly the process by which she overcame this affliction. First, there was a sense of loss. She felt things she loved and were important to her were slipping away — her youth, her beauty, her position. With this loss came grief and sorrow. Grief heals or destroys. It began to destroy her and plunged her into depression where she could just sit in a corner of a room, not caring about anything, and completely escape to another world of illusion — of fantasy.

If this experience has not happened to you, go out of here prepared, for it will happen, you will suffer loss. These stories are not conjured up to illustrate my sermon. These are real people I have known. Some have sat on these very pews, or still do. They have gone through the agonies of grief and sorrow. One of these stories is my own personal experience. Until then I thought grief and sorrow were an abstract something that happened to someone else — but one day it came home to me, and it will come home to you.

I want to talk about how our Christian faith can help us come to grips with grief and sorrow. God does not intend or want us to be defeated, or to live in despair and hopelessness. The good news of Easter is the promise of life — life full and abundant. Regardless of the circumstances of life — you can have a faith that transcends those circumstances and you can be victorious over them. Help is closer than you ever dreamed — for God is here; He is ready to help.

Now, you and I are face to face across the coffee table in my study. We are just talking about this tragic experience that has been yours. I would like to talk about it in three ways:

First of all....

UNDERSTANDING GRIEF

What is grief, this emotion that grips us? Psychologists can give us a great deal of analytical help. Psychology calls grief the wound that heals itself — if it is healthy and normal and there are spiritual resources. Grief is a wound that cuts like a knife. It is painful; there is no denying that pain. Some people try to deny that it even exists, but it is there. If it is a clean wound and not infected, it will heal. But if it is infected, it can plunge you into great despair physically, spiritually, mentally.

So, here is an emotion where we suffer, and the more we suffer, the more it heals us. If there is the expression of grief — the outpouring of grief — if we can shed our tears and tell someone about it — then it has a healing effect upon us.

I am indebted to Dr. John Faucett of Mayo Clinic for this analysis of grief and its process. He says we can observe three stages in grief.

First, there is the impact. When it hits us — suddenly out of a clear blue sky. Some people are just stunned. They cannot react. Others become hysterical. All of us react in our own way, and it does not last long. Our friends say, That one does not really understand what has happened. Certainly, that one does not realize

73

the finality of it. But there is impact.

Then, secondly, there comes the actual healing period which is called recoil and reaction. We recoil from it — then we react to it. Recoil and react. This takes a while, like the wound that takes a while to heal. A long time, sometimes.

For example, there is the total denial of what has happened. It is not so! That person is not dead, they are just in another room. Or, it is not final. My mate has not married someone else. He/she will come back from that other person. The denial of the loss.

Then there are waves of emotional physical stress of weeping for long periods of time. We bounce out of it, and then we weep again — no cause except, maybe, we see someone holding hands. We see one showing affection to another and we suddenly go into these convulsive feelings of grief and sorrow.

There are reactions of bitterness and hostility — reactions to God — God, where are you! How could you do this to me? Reaction to others — hostility and bitterness pushing those who love you away from you. And the reaction of self-condemnation and guilt — What have I done? We think of the harsh things that were said and done and say, If I could just go back and undo those ... but you cannot.

Why did I insist on the operation? Or, why did I let my son go on that trip; he was killed on that trip! And we pass the guilt on to ourselves.

There is only one way for guilt to be removed. There is only one power that can come into a human heart and cleanse the guilt of all the yesteryears. You cannot change yesterday. It is by the grace, love and forgiveness of God expressed through Jesus Christ. You cannot get rid of guilt, any kind, for any cause, unless you come before God and Jesus Christ and say,

God, forgive me. Christ died for me; He took my guilt into His body.

If it is a spiritual experience, a healthy emotional experience; you recoil and react, then you begin to back away from your emotional dependence upon the one that is gone.

The third stage: Rehabilitation. You can become a new person; God gives you new life and a new beginning and you can go on. Because life must go on — it will go on and you have to live it. God wants to help you live it victoriously. And move you on to a better life beyond the experience of sorrow.

That is what we must say about grief. Now, let's apply it.

HOW TO HELP OTHERS

How can we help someone else who is experiencing sorrow? I say to you honestly, I don't know what to say. You are going to the funeral home — what shall I say? I don't know what to say.

Don't say: I understand. That person's inner reaction, whether they tell you or not, is: How can you understand? This hurt is so deep, you cannot understand how I feel inside; nobody can understand. Don't say that, it doesn't help.

So, what you do is say, I love you — I'm here beside you. And be a good listener. Encourage them to talk — to show their emotions. Let them idealize that loved one and tell about the wonderful experiences they had. There is therapy and spiritual value in recapturing the good memories that might crowd out the negatives.

Then help them face life. Get busy. Come on, let's get started doing something. Dr. Karl Menninger of the Menninger Clinic says worthwhile activity is perhaps the single best cure.

75

Third: *Share your faith.* It is a wonderful opportunity to share with someone, in this time of their greatest need, what a vital personal Christian faith can mean. They are hungry; they are reaching out. It is a chance for you to say, Let me pray with you — let me talk with you.

One of the richest moments I have is when I stand before a casket with my arms around the loved ones to pray together. We thank God for the promises and the assurances we have. There is no other place you can turn except to God. There is no other place we can find the affirmations of our faith than in the Lord God. Jesus said, I am the resurrection and the life: He that believeth on me, shall not die.... Let not your heart be troubled ... I go to prepare a place for you....

But, it is all academic until now, isn't it? How do we help others — how do we analyze grief — what is the process?

But then, the real question and issue is: What do you do —

WHEN YOU SUFFER LOSS

It is when that double bed is suddenly single. There are those long nights of loneliness. The telephone is unanswered — someone else has always jumped to answer it — they don't come because they are not there.

When the table is not set. Or there is an empty highchair — a visible reminder that little one is gone. Or, the announcement says that one you lost and thought maybe would come back, is marrying again. It comes home to you; something precious to you has died. What will you do?

What not to do: First of all, don't feel sorry for yourself. Don't complain. Don't tell others how terrible

76

life is — how burdened you are because this has happened to you. You are not the only one to whom pain, suffering and sorrow comes. All of us experience this, one way or another.

In one framework or another, we all will go through this as we go through death. We will lose our loved ones if we live long enough — either parents or children or mates and, certainly, friends. It will happen. Self-pity is the worst thing in the world. That is destructive. That infects the wound. It will not heal as long as you feel sorry for yourself.

And then — don't lock yourself up with your sorrows and your grief and deny the reality of them to make believe that they don't exist.

Here is a family I love very dearly — a professional man and his wife — very active in the church — three fine teenage children — two daughters who were students at UK. The son was in the war and did not come back.

The death of that son so shook this mother and father that they refused to accept the reality of it and finality of it. His room was exactly as it had been when he left — all his personal effects out. The room was dusted every day, and every day mother sat before his picture and wept. The father stood at the door and wept. They shut themselves up in their sorrow — they died spiritually and emotionally. They withered up — they lost life. That is not what God wants you to do!

What you should do: First of all, express your grief. Go ahead, cry about it. Everything I understand about grief — from the scriptures to the psychiatrist — says, Express your grief. To repress it is bad. The Bible says, Weep with those who weep, and rejoice with those who rejoice. Don't be ashamed — don't be afraid to share your grief, express your grief, articulate your grief.

77

Then, having done that — begin to look to tomorrow, for God has given you a tomorrow. You are grieving because someone else lost their tomorrow; but God has given it to you as a gift, you have a responsibility, a stewardship, for the life you have. Believe in the providence of God, that God has kept you and given you tomorrow to do something with it. Do not waste it in self-pity. Do not wallow in sorrow and grief, but say, I must get on my feet and go on. I must do something with my tomorrow.

We quote so often Romans 8:28; *For we know that all things work together for good to them that love God, and are called according to His purpose.* I received a new insight on that.

I saw a US naval vessel in port in Florida. A massive gray ship — overwhelming in size.

I thought — everything about that ship would sink. Taken by itself, a propeller would sink — that huge anchor, drop it over and it would sink — the engines would sink — massive steel plates, the guns — all of these things would sink. But, take all of those things that would sink and put them together into a ship and it floats. Not only does it float, it is going somewhere.

That says to me: Here are all these bitter circumstances of life that come to us. Take any one and it will sink us — we will go right to the bottom! But God can take all of those elements in life, put them together and make it good — it will float — it will go somewhere. God has a purpose for your life. Everything that has happened to you — some bad things — some sorrow and grief were so painful — but God has put it all together to send you somewhere to do something with your life. Look to tomorrow. God gave you tomorrow. You must be a steward of it!

Then, *stand by the church.* In times like these, stand by the church — where you ought to be. It is not

78

a time to withdraw, to retreat. The church is a loving fellowship of caring people — the only fellowship anywhere where people are taken as they are and accepted. You come — others reach out to say, We are here to love you— we are here to care about you. As you come into the fellowship of the church, it helps you; but then you in turn help others.

That is one of the great things about the Singles ministry that I have observed. Those who have suffered terrible accidents on the road of life — the wreck of their marriage and divorce — and scars and suffering. I see people responding to our seminars. And I lead a seminar on the Bible and divorce; we talk about how to begin again. I see them — heads down and withdrawn — despaired — discouraged — the light gone from their eyes. They find fellowship, somebody who cares, a church that accepts them and wants to minister to them. I see a marvelous transformation in their very appearance as they begin to help others. The best counsel and strength comes from someone who has been through the same experience. So, stand by the church.

The last thing: Renew your Christian faith. When sorrow comes — when you suffer loss, your Christian faith really becomes real and meaningful to you. You seem to need God more than ever before — then you find Him greater than ever before.

I quote the promise of the resurrection all the time at funerals. It did not mean as much to me until the day my mother went into the grave and I recalled Jesus said she is alive — she is not here — this is just the old shell.

The promise of reunions with loved ones on the other side did not mean much to me as a young person, But, as time goes by, you begin to say, My faith in the promises of the word of God becomes more meaningful

79

as I see that a six-foot ditch is not the end of life. God has promised me more in Jesus Christ. There is not a relationship we have today in Jesus Christ that can be destroyed by death. Remember that.

Paul said, The last enemy, death itself, has been defeated by the resurrection of Christ. That is the good news of Easter. There is a living Lord; He is in this world today. We can have a personal experience with Him. We can have His presence and power. In a supernatural way, we discover this is not a one-storied world we can see, feel and touch physically. There is a second story, a spiritual story, a spiritual world and there is life in that world. And we can be born again into that world through Jesus Christ.

So, this is a time for you to get a new hold on God and know He is near and real and present. If you suffer loss, God is now here in Jesus Christ to help you and strengthen you.

How do you do that? You make a personal commitment. You open your heart. You give your life — just as when you are married. A young man and woman stand here — how are they married? By two free wills committing themselves each to the other, saying, I do, and they accept each other, and a strange spiritual thing happens. They are joined together as one.

So we come before God and say, I take Jesus Christ. At this time, at this place, I have accepted Him. And something happens. He says, I accept you. In that simple way, we give ourselves to God through Jesus Christ. We are born again, united with Him. He becomes real to us.

QUIT WORRYING AND START LIVING

Psalm 118:24; Matthew 6:25-34

I have a little clipping here from a *TIME Magazine* article; on "Behavior: Polling for Mental Health." It is a $15 million study conducted over six years by the National Institute of Mental Health. They make this startling discovery, contrary to an assumption they had. They have assumed that alcoholism and drugs would be at the top of the list of psychological problems; or if not that, depression. But this study reveals that the number one problem in American society today is anxiety. More than 13.1 million American citizens are afflicted with acute anxiety that is not only making us sick, but even killing us.

The number one cause for suicide is anxiety — that dark heavy cloud of worry that hangs over us. In California some college students are asking the authorities to provide cyanide pills for all students and keep them in storage. So, in the event of a nuclear war, the students can have access to cyanide pills to commit mass suicide and not have to face the reality of life. If this is passed, it will even be a court case to see if the government can legitimately provide ways of suicide in case we face what we think is an impossible future — nuclear warfare. There is a suicide every two minutes somewhere in the United States. The staggering thing is that the largest single age segment is youth — ages 15-24. What is this saying to us?

Anxiety is simply a medical term for plain old worry — that burden of worry that keeps you awake at night — that burden you have — anxiety — worry about what we are going to eat — what we are going to wear — how we are going to live tomorrow and the next day and the next day.

That is exactly what Jesus Christ was talking about here in this scripture. It was the number one concern of the world of that day. It is the number one concern of human personality, regardless of any society or setting. It is the number one problem because we are frail and weak. We are made the victims of time and space. We are made the victims of the temporal, and we are lacking the eternal — we are lacking the security that can come from an attachment to something that is lasting and eternal, that lives above the level of this physical life. And so anxiety is the number one problem, and that is what Jesus was dealing with. Be ye not anxious.... He is saying, quit worrying and start living.

Another clipping puts it in everyday terms.

There are two days in every week about which we should not worry, two days that should be kept free from fear and apprehension. One of these days is *YESTERDAY* with its mistakes and cares, its faults and blunders, its aches and pains. Yesterday has passed forever beyond our control.

All the money in the world cannot bring back YESTERDAY. We cannot undo a single act we performed yesterday — we cannot erase a single word we said. YESTERDAY is gone.

Yet I know a lot of people who live in their yesterdays. I call them the *postmortem people*. Postmortem means after death. Yesterday is dead and buried. We cannot resurrect yesterday.

I know a woman who said to her husband, Why did I ever marry you? They have been married forty years, and she still says, If I had married so-and-so look what

I would have done — where I would have been. That is living in yesterday. You did not marry that other person — you married him. And you are stuck with him today. So — you had better live today and make something out of it because you cannot go back and relive yesterday.

A fellow grumbles on the job. He has been at the job 25 years and he says, I hate my job — I've hated it from the day I started. He lives and stews in this misery when the fact is, he made the choice. Now he has no other choice — so get to living in today! Yesterday is dead. Postmortem people. Some people even say, Why was I ever born? It did not have anything to do with being born; you are born — you are here — you are alive. You cannot do anything about that.

There are those who live in *the yesterdays of their hurts* — the wrongs that have been done to them. I remember what he said about me and I will get even — what she did to me — and I will get my chance one day. So we nurture and carry into today out of yesterday things that happened a long time ago. We carry our grudges, our hostilities and our resentments. Why do we do that?

I can imagine a boy collecting beautiful butterflies to keep and study and enjoy. But I cannot imagine him collecting black widow spiders. I can imagine a little girl being excited about a pet rabbit, but not a rattlesnake. Why keep these poisonous rattlesnakes, and black widow spiders of yesterday in the house of our memories and let them keep pumping venom into today? So we get a little anger going by remembering what he did, she did, what happened — how wronged I have been. That is gone!

Lloyd George, the British statesman, was walking with a friend. As they walked out of the garden, Lloyd George said, Excuse me, and walked back and closed the gate. He remarked, I just make a habit of closing gates. I do not like to leave a gate open after I go through it. That is a good philosophy of life — to close the gate on yesterday and whatever happened. It is dead. If you will close that gate, it will help get the poison out of life that makes us miserable and unhappy today.

I know people who live in *the yesterdays of their sorrows and heartbreaks*, the sufferings they have had. I visited a family who had lost a son in the war many years before, but they showed me his room. It was just as he left it. I found later that they came to that room every day and relived their sorrow and bitterness they had toward God for taking their son from them.

Sorrow is a wound. Grief does come and it is very painful. But God in His grace and mercy heals that wound and lets it be in the past if we let Him. If we keep irritating it and rubbing infection into it we keep it alive and it can hurt us through every day of our life. We have to close the door on yesterday. Yesterday is dead, everything in it has died and we cannot go back and relive it. We cannot bring the dead of yesterday back to life.

Some people live in *the yesterdays of their sins.* They cannot forgive themselves because they cannot believe that God has really forgiven them. They keep saying, I am such a bad person. Oh, the terrible thing I did. They push it into their subconscious, but it keeps coming out because they cannot handle forgiveness. They cannot believe that God is a forgiving, loving God — that the promise of the scripture is that if we confess our sins, He is faithful and just to forgive us our sins and to cleanse us from all unrighteousness.

Jesus admonished, Any man, having put his hand to the plow, and looking back, is not fit for the kingdom.

You will not make it looking back on your sins. The Bible says He removes our sins from us as far as the east is from the west. We ought to come before the cross of Jesus Christ and fall on our knees — Forgive me, Lord, I have sinned — let your forgiveness so come into my life that I shall be cleansed of it all — make me a new person for I believe you took into your body the sins of my life — you died for my sins that you might give me your righteousness and your wholeness and your life. There, before the cross, we can be rid of them as far as the east is from the west.

I like the figure of speech that Dr. Lofton Hudson used. Imagine yourself in a little boat sailing up the river. You are sitting in a deck chair looking back — watching the waves. A rope tied to the boat is pulling a barge. On that barge is all the garbage of yesterday — all the fights and scraps you had with your wife — all the things you have done wrong — all the evil feelings that you have had in your heart. That garbage barge is just piled high with everything that is bad in your life. There it is.

But — that barge is slowing you down — almost stalling the boat — you cannot seem to move against the current. And — you look up and say, Lord Jesus, take this burden off my life — come down and get rid of all this! And Jesus comes. With an axe, he cuts that rope! He cuts it loose and you sit and watch that barge drift down the river with the current, going around the bend and out of sight. And your boat takes off and starts moving against the current, free at last from that horrible barge of garbage that you had been carrying.

And you say it is not only going out of sight, but it is going into the sea and out to the ends of the earth — gone forever as far as the east is from the west. Do you see the beauty of it? Do you see what God promises us? Jesus is saying, Quit worrying and start living! Be free

85

from your sins and your wrongs and your hurts of yesterday.

But — there is a second day. The other day about which we should not worry is *TOMORROW* with its possible adversaries, its burdens, its large promise and poor performance. TOMORROW is also beyond our immediate control. And yet, it is like our yesterdays.

How many of us keep living in our tomorrows — *the tomorrow of procrastination,* for example. You say, Tomorrow I will be a better person. Oh, tomorrow I am going to quit smoking — I know the record on cancer — I know what it is doing to me — I know my age. I am going to quit tomorrow. Tomorrow I am going to start that diet the doctor told me I needed. Tomorrow I am going to be a better husband — a better wife — I am going to make that decision for Christ and His church — tomorrow.

Jesus said a certain rich man had an abundant harvest. He said, Oh, look what I have — I have it made. My barns are already full. I will tear down my barns and build bigger barns and I will bring in my harvest. Then I will sit on my front porch and say, Soul, take thine ease. You have it made for the rest of your life. Jesus said, Thou fool, tonight thy soul shall be demanded of thee. Who here has been promised tomorrow? Would you stand and say, God has promised me tomorrow? Not one of us could. What right do we have to live in tomorrow? Tomorrow is when I am going to do it. I will do that which is right — that which I ought to do, tomorrow.

I wonder if the black angel of death is looking down this very moment on some fine young person — some good husband — lovely wife — and that person is saying, Well, tomorrow — yes, Brother Dehoney, tomorrow — tomorrow I will become a Christian — tomorrow I will start tithing — tomorrow I will join the church. I am a

Christian and I am going to start making my life count. Tomorrow I will do it. I promise God tomorrow. The black angel of death laughs and says, What a fool — this night I shall ride down and take tomorrow from you.

That is not imagination — that is what Jesus said. To anyone who feels this compulsion that I ought to do the right thing now I ought to take this stand — I ought to for God's sake, for other's sake, for my sake — I ought to — and you do not do it and say, I will though, I ought to, I plan to — it is the right thing, I agree — but it will be tomorrow — Jesus said, You are a fool. You cannot live in tomorrow. The tomorrow of procrastination.

And the tomorrow of worry — the things that are going to happen tomorrow. We are living in a good world to produce worriers. In the election, the Democrats are worried to death. The Republicans are even more worried about what will happen. Everybody is worried.

Look at the stock market. Why, you read the articles in the *Wall Street Journal* — today the market went down! And they are worried about inflation. The next day the headlines read, Inflation Licked! But then the stock market goes down again. However, we have the explanation. They are worried about deflation now.

Everybody worries. The rich worry because they have money and they are afraid they will lose it — the poor worry because they do not have any money. The educated worry because they know so much to worry about — the ignorant worry because they do not know what is going on. Religious people worry because they have been saved and they are afraid they will lose their salvation — irreligious people worry because they do not have any salvation to worry about. Young people worry about facing life; old people worry about facing death.

Let me tell you — we are not born worriers. It is not natural for us to worry; you have to learn how to worry. It is an acquired skill — you have to practice at it — and some people practice all the time. I had a Sunday School superintendent who came to lunch every Monday saying, We got problems, pastor, we got problems. Ninety percent of the things he worried about never happened, but that did not keep him from worrying.

Jesus has something to say to us about that: Look at the lilies of the field — look at the birds of the air — look at God's world around you — God is in this world. And if He is in that physical world around you, how much more so is He going to be in this little world inside you! If He cares for that world out there, how much more does He care about you!

So — there are two days about which we need not worry — yesterday and tomorrow. That leaves only one day — TODAY. Any man can fight the battles of just one day. It is only when you and I add the burdens of those two awful eternities — YESTERDAY and TOMORROW — that we break down.

It is not the experience of today that drives us mad — it is remorse or bitterness for something which happened YESTERDAY, and the dread of what TOMORROW may bring. Therefore, let us live but one day at a time. That is exactly what the Bible says. The Psalmist said, This is the day that the Lord hath made; let us rejoice and be glad in it!

Live in this day! That is the only day you can live in, anyway. We decided you could not live in yesterday — you could not live in tomorrow — so this is the day! When you opened your eyes this morning, God gave you a brand new day! That is the only gift He has given you — this day. Live your best in it and when the end of the day comes you will be able to close your eyes and

88

say, Lord l have done the best I can with the gift of this day.

I heard about the grandfather clock that had a nervous breakdown. It had been standing in the hall for two generations ticking two ticks a second. But one day it just went to pieces. He went to the psychiatrist who said, What is your problem? I just could not take the burden any longer. I tick two ticks a second — that is 120 ticks every minute, 7200 ticks every hour! And that is 172,000 every day, a million two hundred nine thousand ticks every week, 62 million ticks a year! I don't think I can do 62 million ticks a year from now on. It's too much!

The psychiatrist said, Let me ask you one question — how many ticks do you have to tick at a time? One. Well, go back and quit worrying — Just think about one tick at a time. At last report, the clock had been ticking away for 50 years.

We all keep trying to tick tomorrow today — trying to second guess God and say, I don't know how the Lord is going to solve that problem. I believe He is there but I don't know how He is going to do it. We worry ourselves sick. It is the Lord's day. Tomorrow is just as much God's day as today. This is the day!

You wake up this morning with a burden — with a care — with anxieties. You have sin — you have a life all messed up. God is here to say, This is the day that the Lord has made for you to do something about. Live this day. Live it to the fullest of your inspiration, your vision, the touch of the Holy Spirit in your heart — do it today — that is when you will stop worrying and start living!

A boy was helping his daddy fix the closet at night. He said, I am out of nails, Son, run out there to the garage and bring me some more nails. It's dark, Daddy. I will get you a light. He gave him the flashlight and said, You will find them on the second shelf. The boy shined the light against the bank of darkness. Daddy, it's dark and I can't see — I can't see the garage. Shine the light down at your feet, son — and step into the circle of light, a step at a time. The boy did that and went all the way down there and all the way back, stepping into the light.

That is exactly what Jesus is saying. This is the circle of day and I have my light and life in this day with you. I am with you. I will never leave you nor forsake you. I am here. Here is the light of my power with you today. Now — step into the light — step into the circle. Suddenly — you discover, with each step you take, there is the light just ahead of you — and you can walk a day at a time.

So — the light is here, shining for you.

THE TRUMPET OF DISCONTENT

Jeremiah 6:10-17

When I was growing up, every boy had a pocket knife that was very special. I still carry a knife with me. And, as I think about this knife, it is a lot like life — like my subject. THE TRUMPET OF DISCONTENT. Discontent is something like this knife. Life thrusts discontent at us; if we seize it by the blade, it cuts us. But if we seize it by the handle, it serves us.

That is exactly what I want to talk about — the trumpet of discontent that sounds in our lives, sooner or later, to make us utterly miserable with life — or, seizing it by the handle, we let it serve us and help us go on to greater things.

Maybe I can illustrate by an incident that happened in Jackson, Tennessee. A man who was a member of another denomination began watching our services on television and then visited our church. One day I said to him, What about your decision about your life — your church membership — I am confident you are a Christian. Oh, yes. I said, You are coming down here — why don't you make a commitment to the Lord and to the church and be a part of our fellowship? He said, Well, I wouldn't have any difficulty — I agree with Baptist doctrine. I like the fellowship of your church. But, you Baptist preachers are all alike. I said, What do you mean?

He said, You preach and holler and you just get me all upset with myself. I come away feeling so guilty — I feel all stirred up. I don't come to church to be made

WHEN LIFE GOES TO PIECES

to feel that way. I have been beat up all week long —
and I come to church where I can settle down
comfortably and get some peace of mind. I don't want
somebody stirring me up — making a lot of demands on
my life. And you make demands that make me
uncomfortable!

Now, does he speak for any of us regarding this
strange paradox of the gospel itself? That is what it is
— for the gospel of Jesus Christ does promise us
comfort and peace to the storm-tossed life. You can
come in from out there and settle down and find such
comfort, peace, satisfaction and ease. Yet, at the same
time, if you really face it honestly and openly, the
gospel of Jesus Christ makes you so uncomfortable, so
discontented, so stirred up that you say, I can't have
any peace — I can't be comfortable.

But that is what Jesus said: My peace I give unto
you. Then, in the next breath almost, he said, I come
not to bring peace but a sword — a knife — that will
cut, sever and break relationships and keep you all
stirred up.

That is what this prophet Jeremiah was talking
about 2700 years ago. God says, I have set watchmen
over you saying, Hearken to the trumpet of discontent.
Get stirred up. He is trying to get you dissatisfied — to
shake you out of your lethargy and comfort and ease.
Listen to the trumpet of discontent. But they said, Let
us alone — we will not listen.

There is no peace of mind with the trumpet of
discontent. Jeremiah did not want the people of his
day to be contented and satisfied. In fact, he was called
the wailing prophet — he was preaching despair; he
was stirring them up.

THE SITUATION

I wonder if you can see any parallel in this story. First of all, Jeremiah says there was great prosperity. Everybody was making money. He says, They are just consumed with covetousness, materialism, the getting and grasping. They hold on to things. That describes life for us today. Get ahead — get it — grab it — this consumes all our energies.

Jeremiah says, secondly, there is great immorality, abominations. The word, abomination, is more than immorality — it is horrible, gross immorality. It is so commonly accepted the people have lost their capacity even to blush.

Does that describe us today? Is anybody embarrassed by the common language we have in conversation that used to be locker-room language? Does anyone ever come out of a movie blushing at the immorality and language — or say of a book, I cannot read this book — it is shocking?

Does anyone blush over the gross immorality of sexual perversions — the complete discarding of marriage as a stable institution? Shack up together on a college campus— have a child without a legal spouse — that is all right. We are more open today, more honest — we don't blush about it any more. Jeremiah said that was the condition then! Isn't this as relevant as the morning paper?

Then — they had a *pseudo-religion* of ritual and form. Everybody said, We go to church — we go to the temple. But it was not vital and personal; it had not changed their lives.

Finally, they were saying, *peace, peace.* Don't worry — God is not going to let anything happen to this His nation. We are His people; all is well. Even at that moment Jeremiah said the enemy was ready to come

93

down, and the enemy will be the instrument of God's judgment upon the people of that day.

Haven't we been saying — God will not let anything happen to Christian America? We are His people in this world. Suddenly, we see in the Moslem world — in Iran — a wave of hatred we can hardly cope with. They are talking about dying as martyrs to stamp out this satanic force called America. We suddenly realize they have us by the throat and there is nothing we can do. We are beginning to say, maybe there is no peace — maybe we are in trouble — maybe something will happen to us.

The trumpet of discontent is sounding in the circumstances of life today. God says, Wake up and get disturbed. It is like my knife — seize it by the blade and it cuts us, destroys us. Take the handle and see the value of discontent and what it can do for us.

Look — first of all —

PROGRESS

All human progress has come as a result of discontent. Only when we become dissatisfied, discontented, do we move to something higher. A struggle against the situation, the status quo, to rise to something. Man carried a heavy load on his back in primitive times. He became discontented with that burden on his back, so he tied two poles together, put the burden in the middle of the X — and drug that burden — and discovered it was lots easier.

Then one day he saw a wild animal — I could put this on that animal if I could catch him. So the horse was domesticated. Discontented with that horse dragging those poles, he invented a sled and found that horse could carry a larger load. Discontented with the sled, he put wheels on it and made a wagon. Still discontented, man put an engine in that wagon and made a horseless carriage called a car.

Then, discontented with a car that could go just 90 miles an hour down the freeway, he put wings on that wagon with an engine and made an airplane that could fly as fast as sound. Discontented with things like they are causes us to want a better way. All scientific progress comes this way — discontented hearts saying, I want to discover new truth — more truth.

Paul Sabatier, a French organic chemist, received the Nobel Prize in 1912 for his work on the nitrogen atom. He had arrived — he had achieved — he had it made. But the restless spirit, the trumpet of discontent, so stirred within him that he continued studying and experimenting. When he died in 1941 they found on his desk and in his laboratory experiments that would have required 200 years for him to complete! But, he was still pressing on because something was stirring inside him saying, It's not enough — I must keep going!

SPIRITUAL MORAL

This is true in the moral and spiritual realm also. It is only when discontent stirs us with what we are and the way things are that we press on to a better life and a better way.

William Lloyd Garrison, an Abolitionist, began as a young man fighting for a cause. He looked into the face of a black slave and saw the face of God. And he said, This is not right to enslave and degrade a human creature, a child of God like this. And he began the battle that split a country. There were times when he was jailed for his views; and then there were times when he was jailed for protection against the wild crowds that would have killed him. He was one of the instrumental factors that brought about the destruction

95

of that horrible institution called slavery. When we look at racial discrimination and economic depravity because of injustice, it is then that the trumpet of discontent stirs us to say, Rise up and do something about it.

Contentment is a force within us that pulls us back and says, Let us alone — maintain the status quo — don't rock the boat — be careful. But the prophet says, Listen to the trumpet and answer its call! You cannot stand still when the trumpet of discontent is sounded from the lips of Christ Himself from the pages of the gospel.

It is true in our church life. The trumpet of discontent is a stagnant pool of selfish contentment in a Sunday school class that says, We are satisfied — let us alone — don't stir us up. We do not need any more people. We are happy with whom we have and what we are doing.

A church may say, We have arrived! Look right here — this sanctuary is packed. Why should we do any more to reach anybody else. Look at the vast programs we have. I want to say there is the tendency for us to settle down in comfort, feeling we have done it all— now let's sit back and enjoy it. Oh, how God is sounding the trumpet of discontent in the hearts of church members today saying, Let's go on to greater things. Now is no time to be at ease in Zion.

This is true in *our personal life*. There is a force, a voice, in this world that says, Let me alone — I am all right — I have accepted Christ — I am a member of the church — I live a good life — I don't beat my wife — I don't steal from my employer — I am a good person. Any time we become so satisfied with ourselves, something inside us dies. It is death for us when we say, I have made it, spiritually.

Some time ago I saw a documentary on Pompeii.

96

When Vesuvius erupted, the volcanic ash caught that town of Pompeii just as they were — people in their shops, on the streets. A man fleeing with his dog — the lava and ash just trapped and froze him. When his body decayed inside that cold lava, it left a hollow form. They have poured plaster of paris into that form and he is recast just as he was 2,000 years ago.

That is what happens to us with satisfaction and contentment; it freezes us as we are. How would you like for God to say, Stay like you are right now — never be any better, any different — never change any circumstance in your relationships at home, with others, or with God. Contentment freezes us and kills us like we are. It is the trumpet of discontent that calls out to us: Change! Rise up.

CONQUEST

How does this trumpet of discontent wake us up? How can it change us? Let me use an old-time, old-fashioned word called *repentance*. A good word. Repentance means two things:

First of all, repentance means *to stand in front of God's searching* eye, his mirror, *and see ourselves as we really are.* That is the first dimension of repentance. And when I am really honest and level with myself, I back away saying, I'm terrible. I am a sinner. I am wicked.

Jeremiah said, That is the problem with the people of my day — they see their abominations and they do not even blush. They are not even bothered with how they look.

A person said, I can't get any peace — I am so torn up I just cannot get things settled in my life. I replied, No, and you won't get any peace — because you are doing wrong. You look in that mirror and see God's dissatisfaction with you — and you are dissatisfied with yourself. Until you determine you are going to be different and changed — there will not be any peace for you. Repentance is first — being honest enough to look at ourselves in God's mirror and see ourselves as we are.

Secondly, *repentance is to look to Christ and see ourselves as we may become.* His grace and forgiveness call us on — you do not have to stay like you are — you can change — you can be forgiven — cleansed — made over again — you can become somebody.

CONTENTMENT?

But you say, You are still talking about the trumpet of discontent. Isn't there any contentment? Isn't there some time when that trumpet quits blasting and I can settle down a little bit? I say, No —no. But let me share some discoveries as we deal with this.

The first discovery is: *real contentment is not in arriving, but in striving.* If I were to have another title for this sermon, it would be, STRIVING OR ARRIVING. Which would you rather be — striving or arriving? Most of us would rather arrive — get it all made — get it all in order. But we suddenly discover when we get there, that is when we really become miserable. There is no contentment in saying, Soul, take thine ease — I am all that I ought to be and have all that I ever want — I am settled. The real joy in life comes in striving, the struggle, the upward march — to higher things.

Let me use two examples: The rich young ruler came to Jesus. Master, what must I do to inherit eternal life? He was searching — he knew he lacked something. But when the master pressed him, he found he did not lack anything. The master said, Son, you know the commandments. The young man said, Yes, Lord, I have observed all of those since my youth. I have arrived, spiritually — there is not a bad thing in my life — I keep the law — cross every T — I am a pretty good fellow.

Well, he was rich—he had arrived. A ruler — a leader in the synagogue — he had prominence. He said, Lord, I have really got it made — I am on top of it all — I have it all together in life. But — I still want eternal life.

The Lord said, Put all of this aside — that is not where you will find your joy. Take up your cross and begin to struggle with me — climb that hill to Calvary with me. The young man said, I don't want to keep on striving, I am tired. And the scripture says. He went away sorrowful.

Now, in contrast, here is the Apostle Paul — a man who was beaten, shipwrecked, suffered all kinds of things. He never did arrive in this world — he never had it made — he never got it all together. But, as he came toward the end of his life, he kept saying, Joy, joy, rejoice, rejoice! He was God's troubadour singing his song across the pages of history, and across the face of Asia and Europe. Rejoice — let your joy be known! But then he says, My song is not in attaining, but in striving.

In Phil. 3:13-14 he says, Brethren, I count not myself to have attained — but this one thing I do, forgetting those things which are behind, and reaching forth unto those things which are before, I press toward the mark.... I am still struggling toward that high calling of God in Christ Jesus — and I will keep on climbing and pressing until the last breath leaves my body. That is what gives me a song — and gives me joy.

And I say — you cannot find joy in life until you begin to say, I am pressing on — I am going to rise higher. I am going to struggle, even in this moment, and go out a notch higher in my life — I am going to make a commitment that moves me further along — morally, spiritually — in my relationship with God and

His church.

Put it this way: We are climbing a ladder. Some are way down here — some are midway — some are way up here. Now, we are to find no pride in where we are on that ladder. You cannot say, I am way up here — above all the rest of you. The Lord says we are not to pass that kind of judgment. Some of those still on the lower rungs struggle against temptations you never knew. We came from a different background that you never had. Maybe we have a marital problem that you never faced. We have habits you never had — they never bothered you. So we are weak but we are struggling — still climbing up the ladder, and we have gotten this far. The Lord says the measure is not where you are on the ladder — it is whether you are still climbing!

Are you still climbing? Still striving? Still pressing on? Then the Lord says, Well done, thou good and faithful servant. It is like climbing a rope; if that rope is tight, you are still climbing; if the rope is slack, you have stopped.

So it is not in attaining the top — it is in striving that we find our song, even the song of salvation — when we repent and confess our sins and give ourselves to Jesus Christ, saying, I want to be a Christian. I don't see the end. I see that as the beginning of a glorious pilgrimage as I strive and grow into the very likeness of Christ Himself.

WHY BAD THINGS HAPPEN TO

GOOD PEOPLE

John 9:1-7

There is a best seller entitled, *WHEN BAD THINGS HAPPEN TO GOOD PEOPLE*, written by Harold Kushner, a Jewish rabbi. It has some gaps in it which is understandable since he comes from a different perspective than I. But this is a question asked by all of us sooner or later. This was the first question asked of me as a minister, and I did not quite know how to handle it.

My first funeral was for a nine-year-old boy that was killed on a bicycle. He had ridden it out of the hollow onto the Goodlettsville highway going into Nashville — the car hit him and he was killed instantly. Standing over that casket his widowed mother asked again and again, Why? Why did this happen to him? He was a Christian. Why?

I guess it will be the last question I am asked. It is about the most relevant question of the moment — whether it was yesterday or last week — as we stand with a daughter beside her mother with needles in her arms and crying out in pain. With tears in her eyes she says, Why does God let her stay like this? Why must she suffer so — why can't she just go on? The first question and the last question — the continuous question — the ageless question.

Job, sitting on an ash heap — had lost his family — his flocks — his money — his health — and he cries out to God. I have tried to serve you and honor you — I have lived right — why do the heathen, the godless, prosper and the righteous suffer like this? Why? Maybe it is even the last question Jesus asked. He hung on the cross and he cried out, My God, my God, why hast thou forsaken me?

Being a Christian intensifies the question. If I could come from the perspective of the Jewish rabbi, it might not be a hard question to answer. But being a Christian, I have an understanding of God that is different. I understand God to be the Father who loves so much that He sent His Son who died on the cross for me. He has this personal interest in me to such an extent that if all the rest of the world had been saved, and I had been the only lost person in this world, He would still have sent His Son to die for me. And with a belief in that kind of God, it becomes even more difficult for me to understand — if God is like that and I am His child and I am a Christian — how can bad things happen to good people like me?

From the beginning, we ought to get a clear under-standing of our promise from God and from Christ. Read the scripture — Jesus Christ, in all His teaching, never promised that if we would follow Him, we would never suffer. He never did say, Follow me and no bad things will ever happen to you. He never said, Be good Christian parents— establish a Christian home — live right — do right — teach Sunday School — tithe — and I promise you that you will have a perfect family — nothing bad will ever happen to you or your children in that home. He never said, Be a good man — a righteous man — a godly man — serve the Lord — honor Him in your business — be Christlike in your dealings and you will never lose any money — you will never have any hard times — you will never have disappointment — you will always have successes in business enterprises.

102

In fact, Jesus said, If you follow me, I will send you out like sheep among wolves. That is pretty tough. He said, You will have tribulation. It is the way of the cross, even. Be of good cheer for I have overcome the world. I send you out not to find peace, but a sword. It will be warfare — it will be hard. Narrow is the way — steep is the path. It is a hard way.

So — let me start by telling you three *wrong answers* to Why! The first — *all suffering happens to us because of sin*. We have sinned and sin brings suffering. The disciples thought that in this passage I read. They pointed to that man born blind and said, Somebody sinned or he would not be blind. Lord, is he blind because he sinned, or is he blind because his parents sinned and visited upon him their sins? Jesus answered, No — you cannot relate the two — you cannot say — because he is blind, that proves somebody committed a great sin — he or his parents. In fact, he said, I will use his blindness to glorify God — it is a part of my work and ministry. And Jesus healed him.

In Luke 13:1-5 we find this incident. The disciples said, Lord, you hear about that terrible thing that happened in Galilee? While some Galileans were in the synagogue offering the sacrifice, Pilate's soldiers came in and slaughtered them and their blood was mixed with the blood of the sacrifice! What terrible sinners they must have been for such a terrible thing to happen! Jesus said, No — that terrible thing happening to them does not prove they were terrible sinners any more so than when that tower of Siloam fell and killed eighteen people. Those people were not any worse sinners than those who were not killed — or any worse sinners than you are.

The Jews said if something terrible happened to you, that proves you have done a terrible sin. And we have a tendency to say that today. A woman said, What have I done to deserve this? What did I do to God to make Him do this to me? I said, You have not done anything — God is not punishing you with the bad things that are happening to you.

We do not deny there is some relationship between sin and suffering. All sin will bring suffering somewhere to somebody, but not all suffering is due to sin directly. The reverse is not true. My philosophy professor at Vanderbilt University said, "Watch your logic that it does not slip. You can go from general to the particular, but you cannot go backward. For example, you can say all greyhounds are dogs but you cannot reverse it and say that all dogs are greyhounds." You can say all sin does bring suffering, but not all suffering is due to sin.

Secondly, *neither can you say, God sent suffering upon me.* God is not the author of suffering and tragedy. In fact, Jesus clearly repudiates this. He looked at the woman and said, Behold this one whom Satan hath bound for eighteen years.... And He healed her. He said Satan did this to her — God did not do it. And God does not do it. But there is a permissive will of God that allows bad things to happen to us. I want you to remember three words.

The first word is *ignorance,* the second word is *folly;* the third word is *sin.* We have ignorance and folly and sin in our lives. God wants to *replace our ignorance with knowledge.* He wants our *folly to be replaced by wisdom.* And He wants *our sin to be replaced by righteousness.* And, in the process of life, we go through this experience whereby God, in His permissive will, allows some bad things to happen to us to help us come from ignorance to knowledge — from folly to wisdom — and from sin to righteousness.

Here is a story to illustrate. Here is an indulgent mother — a widow who has an only son. She indulges

104

him to a fault. She spends her days and nights trying to make him happy and to give him anything he wants if it will make him happy. He wants a car and finally she says, When you can get a driver's license, I will buy you a new car — and she does. He drives that car like a maniac. He likes to take the corners on two wheels — he likes to scratch off and leave rubber 25 feet on the pavement. And she is happy because she has made him happy, giving him what he wants.

One day he does not make the corner. There is a telephone pole and, bang! He hits that pole, crumples his car and is carried to the hospital with a broken leg and cuts and bruises — he is painfully bruised up — not killed, but all beat up. At the hospital the mother is standing over his bed when the pastor comes in. She wails, Oh, pastor, why did God do this to me? He said, He did not do it to you — he did it to him. Then, Why did God do this to him? The pastor said, God did not do it to him — he did it to himself.

Well, why didn't God get that telephone pole out of the way? Why did He let him hit that pole? He was going too fast — he could not make the curve. And if God is in the business of pulling up telephone poles in front of wild reckless drivers and putting them somewhere else, then He might put it in the middle of the highway where I would hit it. God does not pull up telephone poles to save those who are ignorant and foolish and, in their folly, driving too fast. God, in His permissive will, let him hit that telephone pole — and He is going to let him lie in that bed with a broken leg and suffer for about two weeks. He is going to help him replace that ignorance with a little knowledge about how fast you ought to drive — and replace the folly with a bit of wisdom and judgment — and replace the sin of careless driving that might kill somebody, including himself, with righteousness. We do not say

105

that God did this to us — but God does allow some things to happen to us because He is trying to replace ignorance with knowledge to help us learn — folly with wisdom to help us be wiser in our choices — and replace sin with righteousness.

A third wrong answer is actually a pagan answer. They say, *Bad things and suffering come by chance.* This is a world of chance. It is a world of fate. Soldiers went into the war saying, I am not worried — I am not afraid — I believe there is a bullet with my name on it — and when that bullet comes, there is nothing I can do.

Or, I am just a Hardshell Baptist — I am just a Presbyterian who believes in predestination. When my time comes, it will come; if I am going down the highway or sitting in a chair at home, it is going to come — that is fixed. That is pagan fatalism — that is not Christian. No — it is not due to chance either.

Let's turn it around and see if we can get some positive answers. I suggest three *positive answers* about why. As we read the scripture here, we see three things.

First, we see that *suffering and hardship and difficulties can be purposeful.* They are not inflicted upon us for no purpose at all. So — what is God's purpose for us? It is not for us to sit in comfort and luxury and ease all the time. If that were His purpose, just get some hypodermic needles and a high-powered drug and give everybody a shot so they would have no pain at all. You would not have any anxieties or worries. But you could not have any joys either. You could not have any stimulation of your mind or any of the other attributes of human personality. You see, we mistake God's purpose for our living. He did not put us here to twiddle our thumbs and say, I am so happy — nothing bothers me — nothing ever will. No — God put us here to grow — to aspire in life to the likeness of Jesus

106

Christ — to grow unto His stature. And growth comes hard and difficult — by exercising — by trial and testing.

And that leads me to the second positive answer. *Suffering and bad things are disciplinary.* They exercise a discipline upon us. No pain, no gain. The athlete said, There is no real gain until I get to the pain of that extra exhaustion— when I push those weights that last time in pain, only then am I growing muscles — when I run that race until I get the pain of exhaustion and overcome that; then I get that second wind. And that is true in life — no cross, no crown, is the spiritual application of that. Disciplinary.

Let me use an example. You as a father have high ambitions for your son — you want him to achieve his best. You are a good father — you love him and you care about him. One day that son says, Dad, I have a confession — I've not been going to school, I've been playing hooky. I haven't been doing my homework at night — I've been playing video games when you thought I was studying. Now, I have to take an examination this semester in mathematics. I don't know it and I am going to fail. And, Dad, look what is going to happen — if I fail mathematics, I can't graduate from high school this year. If I can't graduate this spring, I can't go to summer camp and you have already made the deposit. And I can't go to college next fall. Look at all these things that are going to happen to me if I don't pass this exam — what am I going to do?

Well, you are a wonderful daddy and you say, That is all right son, don't you worry — I love you and I want you to be happy. I don't want you to miss going to college or miss summer camp. I want you to pass with flying colors — so here is what I will do — I'm an engineer and I keep up on my math, so I will just take your exam for you. You won't have to worry about it.

107

You say, That is absolutely absurd! Of course it is! And yet, that is exactly what you and I ask our Heavenly Father to do for us all the time. Lord, spare me the disciplines. I would love to be a sweet, wonderful, deep Christian with lots of faith but, Lord, I don't want to go through the disciplines of learning how to be deep in my faith. I want to have power in prayer, but I don't want to have to go through the valleys of the shadow to learn what prayer can mean. When I read my Bible, I understand it this way — these things happen to us for disciplinary purposes. We can grow every time something bad happens — it is a chance to grow.

But Paul gives a third positive answer: Even *the worst of bad things are temporary*. They are passing. But I still have not gotten to the bottom line.

Why do they happen? The answer is simply this: We do not know why. He does not spell it out for us — one, two, three, four — exactly why that happened to you. Even if I gave that answer to you, would you be any better off? Would that enable you to live with it, be victorious over it? We do not need answers. We need power! We need the power that helps to live above it. That is why Jesus said, In this world ye shall have tribulation — but be of good cheer — I have overcome the world. And He will give us the power to overcome it. That is what is promised.

So I give you three rules: First of all, *expect bad things*. It is a part of this world in which we live — a sinful world full of accidents and violence and evil. And in this world we shall have tribulation, Jesus said. We will be tossed about — expect it. That is the way the game of life is going to be played.

Your boy says, Dad, I want to play football. Are you sure? Yes sir! I want to carry that ball over the goal line in front of a crowd of 30,000 — everybody will stand up and cheer and call my name. If you are going to play the game, here is the price. You have to go out for practice and you will be knocked about and bruised up and so sore that some nights you will cry yourself to sleep, you hurt so much. You are liable to get a broken bone. You will have to change your habits — your sleeping and eating. Well, I'm ready! Remember, I told you — I don't want to hear any whimpering from you. Expect it!

The second rule: *Accept it when it comes.* It is not so important *what happens* to us; it is *how we react* that makes the difference. The sun shines on a bowl of butter and melts it. It shines on a chunk of clay and hardens it. The same sun, the same heat, melts the butter and hardens the clay.

Here comes adversity in the family. I have seen it happen again and again to persons in the same family — the same kind of accidents — the same kind of broken bones. And, as it comes, one person is softened and mellowed and made sweeter and their Christian faith is deepened. And the other is hardened and becomes bitter and resentful and cannot cope with life.

Look around— there are a lot worse things happening to other people than to any of us — but they get along better. It is how they react to it. They accept it.

A dear saint of God said, Every time something bad happens to me, I go to my easy chair and sit back and take it easy. What is your easy chair? It is Romans 8:28. That is the promise that says, All things work together for good to them that love God, who are called according to his purpose. When anything goes wrong and I cannot handle it — I just plop myself down in that easy chair and say, Lord, I am here and I just trust you. And it is all right. That is what God has promised — His providence. His good will takes even the worst things that can happen, to us and works them together to make them good. Accept it.

And the third rule: *Use it.* A *Time Magazine* article told of Solzhenitsyn, the Russian, speaking in Britain — calling us back to God as a civilization that is going down, down, down — a world that is going down, down into the vortex of atheism and materialism. He tells his own experience. By the time he was 15 years old, he was a hard Marxist and complete atheist. He challenged the regime in his writings, bringing down the wrath of officials upon him and was sentenced to eight years of hard labor in a lumber camp in the frozen waste of Siberia! He said, I was sick unto death — mortally ill. It was then I found God anew and afresh — in the concentration camp of Siberia.

He gained a power and a strength that enabled him to overcome not only the persecution and the hardships, but he became a Nobel Prize winner and world figure outside of Russia to confront communism and atheism in the world today. He let adversity bring him to God! He used it.

And every one of us can say, Lord, I want this bad experience to help me know you better and get closer to you. Lord, I trust you to work it out.

That is the message — let us apply it. Do you have Christ in your heart — are you committed to Him? Have you turned it over to Him? Can you rest in that easy chair that all things can work together because you love God — that your life is ordered according to His purpose and will?

If you cannot do that, make a decision for Christ.

COPING WITH LONELINESS

John 16:32-33

I stood beside a casket as the man broke into sobs and fell across the casket and cried out, I am alone — I am alone — I am all alone now. His wife had just died — he had no family left. They had all died — there were no children. There he was — in a crowded funeral home among many friends and neighbors; but he was crying out of that essential loneliness of the human heart, I am alone! I am alone — all alone!

The wedding was a high hour of celebration when the last child was married. The couple, with a bit of sadness, said to each other, Well, we are back where we started — all alone. The loneliness of the empty nest and the children gone. All alone.

The police were called to come to an apartment where a lonely woman had lived for many years. She had no relatives. She was dead. They came in and began to sort her belongings. They found a diary that she had kept; and the whole nation wept as they read the news reporter's story about her diary.

On every day for the last year, there was a single phrase written: No one came today. No one came today. For more than a year she had sat in that apartment, lonely and sick, waiting just for a knock on the door, for the telephone to ring, for someone to come. And no one came.

The little girl cried herself to sleep at night. Her mother said, What is the matter? I am lonesome — I want my daddy. A great pang of sorrow and remorse and guilt sweeps over the mother because there has been a divorce. Daddy is gone — but the pain of loneliness is still there for the little girl. She knows not what the problems were or why the marriage did not work — but she is so lonely for her daddy.

Paul Tournier, a Swiss medical doctor, writer and theologian wrote a book on this, *ESCAPE FROM LONELINESS*. In that book he makes this point: The most prevalent malady today, throughout all society, is loneliness. The common pain of the whole body of humanity — all ages, all stratas of life, all levels economic, social, intellectual — the common pain is loneliness.

THE CAUSE OF LONELINESS

Let us ask this question of the finest minds and authorities that we have: What is the cause of this loneliness? It is so universal and so pervasive. They would say there are a number of factors.

First of all, there are *sociological causes* that contribute to this great loneliness today. They mean simply the way we live — our life styles and our values in life.

For example, they say, the mobility of our society contributes to our aloneness, separation and alienation. That is one of the reasons why a TV series like "The Little House on the Prairie" appeals to all of us. It turns back the pages of time to life like it used to be years ago. Just a little tightknit family and the extended family. They lived together and stayed together. They were in the same community where fathers and grandfathers and great-grandfathers were — roots are there — identity is there — values are there. It is the beautiful story of life like it used to be.

112

And we romanticize and wish we had that kind of security. The biggest venture away from home was to get in the wagon and go to town on Saturday. You did not stay there long. You went right back to that secure and safe and enduring place called home. But it is not like that today. No one lives like that today; that is gone. Sociological changes.

They tell us that 40 million people a year in the United States move and change their residence — go somewhere else. One of the members of our church told me, We have lived in eleven different cities in the last 18 years. What does that do to you — to be uprooted and moved somewhere else to begin all over again?

They say the average American will move 14 times in their lifetime. You may be above that average or below it — but start counting. There are some schools where the turnover is as high as 50 percent within the school year. Those are children that are changed, uprooted, moved about — what does this do to us? It means we have no roots — there are no attachments— there is no safe, secure place. Loneliness comes as a result of this instability.

He have been called the throwaway generation for this reason. Lacking permanence and stability, we begin to use things that we cannot keep; it is impractical to keep them so we just dispose of them. They now have a throwaway graduation robe. We rented ours; but they find they can make them cheaper out of paper that looks like cloth. You buy it and when you are through, wad it up and throw it away. The latest thing is a throwaway wedding gown. Made of paper that looks like fabric, you can use it, then wad it up and throw it away. Why? Who has an attic and a trunk and can put that away for daughters and granddaughters to use? We have to get rid of those things. We do not have those attachments to the past. This is one of the things that

113

has caused our loneliness. Sociological changes. Uprooted.

The girl standing at the desk in the Greyhound Bus Station in Washington, D. C., had gone away to college. Then she had gone to Washington and had a good job there. But she is buying a ticket to leave the crowded city with all its excitement. She is buying a ticket to East Kentucky. They asked her why, and she said, I am going home — home to a little cottage way up at the end of a hollow — far from the county seat even. That is home — and I am so lonesome for home. She was lonely in the crowd of people, but she was lonesome for home up a hollow in the mountains.

Then there are *circumstantial causes.* There are things that just happen to us — circumstances over which we have no control. Life and death. Death is a circumstance that comes to all; and death will come and eventually break every relationship and leave someone lonely.

There is the circumstance of divorce which is the death of a marriage. How many lonely people are left after the breakup of a marriage? And there is the circumstance of poverty that makes people lonely — of physical handicaps. The loneliness of wealth and prominence and leadership. When you are at the top, there is loneliness. Money can buy friends but not the kind of friends that can fill the lonely feeling in your heart.

And, there are *conditions inside our own heart* that make for loneliness. Our own failure — our own sin — our own selfishness — our own pride — our own attitude of arrogance and self-sufficiency — sin itself inside our human heart. Out of that sin comes this sense of loneliness and alienation — even an alienation and loneliness from God whom we know is afar off from us and we are so lonely for Him, if we will admit it.

114

Well, that is the situation. What do we do about loneliness? How do we handle it?

THE WRONG WAY

There are destructive ways of handling loneliness in which we but make the situation worse. These are *the wrong* ways to handle loneliness: One way to handle it is by *anesthetizing the loneliness* — by anesthetizing the pain. You take a shot in the hospital to relieve pain — so we go about the pain of loneliness saying, Give me a quick fix so I can live with this pain.

Then, there are a couple of social institutions that have evolved where people can go and get their pain anesthetized. One we call the neighborhood bar, the cocktail lounge. It is filled with a lot of people who do not like alcohol, they do not like to drink — it is against their morals — they have a conscience about it. But they go there anyway because they can be anesthetized — the pain of their loneliness can be eased a little bit and they will find a bartender who will talk to them. When they get enough anesthetic in them and the barriers are down a little bit more and their inhibitions are washed away, they find someone on a stool next to them who is in the same condition and they begin to be friendly and to talk.

The tragedy is— when that wears off, they are right back where they started. They have used a crutch to solve the problem, and it has not solved a thing; they have just been exploited. Their loneliness has been exploited by those who do it just to make money off of them — and leave them as lonely, or more so, than when they came in.

That is what the cocktail party or the happy hour is all about, too. Come to the happy hour because you are unhappy — you are lonely — you do not know how

115

to talk with people — you feel all alone at work and in the crowd. Get in here at the happy hour — if you get enough anesthetic pumped into you, the pain will go away, and you will find you are happy for a little while. But then the happy hour is over. Seven o'clock comes and you stagger home. You have to face that empty apartment — those lonely walls — those problems of life — and you have not solved a thing. That is the destructive way to handle the loneliness.

Another way that we try to handle our loneliness is just to *run away from it* — to deny it — to so cram and pack our lives with frantic activity— going from one sports event to another — one entertainment to another where there is music and noise and people. If we could just keep busy like this, we could kill the loneliness by running away from it. But it does not work.

The worst way that most of us try to handle it is in *self pity*. We just sit and look at ourselves inside and we get so sorry for ourselves. It is a vicious cycle. We are lonely when we look at ourselves and get self-centered and we dump all our self-pity on ourselves. And the more we pity ourselves, the lonelier we get. Who wants to be around somebody that is always full of self-pity and complaining and bemoaning about how bad things are for them? That makes us worse.

Loneliness makes us bitter and bitterness makes us lonely. Who wants to be around a bitter person all the time? Loneliness makes one jealous; and jealousy makes us lonely. And who wants to be around a jealous person all the time? Loneliness makes us odd — different, strange. And oddness makes us lonely. Nobody wants to be around an odd person.

So this is the cycle. That is the destructive way to handle your loneliness — to look in and feel sorry for yourself. We have to have a power — we have to have something happen in our lives that will break that cycle and get us out of it.

THE RIGHT WAY

Let's look at the positive constructive ways to handle our loneliness. First of all, we must *accept our loneliness* — accept that it is a part of life. We were made as individuals. We were made lonely. We were made a single person and it is a part of the nature of our creation that God made us to be alone. Some things we have to do alone; nobody else can do them for us. We have to be born alone — we have to die alone — no one else can die for us. We have to confess our sins alone; nobody else can do it for us. That does not mean that we do it by ourselves, but no one can do it for us. We have to receive Christ ourselves. No one else can receive Christ for us. We have to enter the kingdom of God for ourselves, by ourselves; no one else can do it for us.

So, it is a part of the very structure of creation. God made us not only to be social beings with others, but He also made us to be a lonely person. Every one must bear his own burden. So, accept it. There is a loneliness that is a part of our nature by creation; accept it. Accept the humanness that is mine and yours.

We are frail, sinful, human beings, living among other frail, sinful, human beings. There are those who will disappoint us. There are those who will break relationships with us. There are those who will misunderstand us; and we will misunderstand them because we are in a sinful world.

We are going to be hurt and disappointed and broken-hearted, again and again. That is a part of the life that God has given us. We can not expose ourselves to rich relationships unless we are willing to run the risk of those relationships being broken. You cannot run the risk of having the joy of marriage without

117

having to run the risk also of the sorrow of separation. They have to come hand in hand and you will get some of both.

So, let us accept our loneliness; we are going to have some. It is unrealistic to believe that you can go through life and not be lonely — many times — oftentimes — sometimes. You will be lonely.

Secondly, *use your loneliness.* God intended for that loneliness to be transformed into something else. He intended for us to use that loneliness to have aloneness, or solitude. How important solitude is for the development of our minds and our spirits and even our bodies.

A missionary in Indonesia said, One of the most depressing things about this society here is the heavy concentration of population. Over a hundred million people in these tiny islands live so close together that people are born and live and die and are never out of the sight of somebody else. Never alone — never able to be alone. That is not normal and natural. God wants us to have these times of solitude.

A girl took her fiance to see her home. They went up a valley to a little mountain home that overlooked a little lake. It was a little unpainted house on the shores of that lake. She said, It is not much — just an humble home — this is where I came from. I want you to come out here and sit on the porch and look out over the lake. This is our home and it is a wonderful place to look out from — across the lake and into the hills beyond.

We all need a place to look out from — a place of solitude whether we go out into nature, or just go into our study — a time when we sit down and transform our loneliness into aloneness and begin to get our values straightened out. We need a retreat where we can go and get our directions, our purposes — to think things through and get a new grip on life.

That is the second constructive way. If you are alone, use it as aloneness — a time for solitude; and let it be a productive time. The greatest works of art, the greatest works of creativity — the greatest works of writing — the greatest works of inventing have been wrought out in solitude. Solitude and aloneness have great value. Learn to appreciate being alone.

Then third: *Transform your loneliness into a blessing* — a blessing to others and a blessing to yourself. A mother sent her little girl to the store to get some groceries. She gave her a list and the money and she went running out the door. But she did not come directly back. Her mother got worried about her. Pretty soon the little girl came — and her mother said, Where are the groceries? I did not get them. Why didn't you get them — what happened? I was worried about you. The girl said, I did not go to the store yet because I was delayed and I knew you would be worried about me; I came back to tell you. What in the world happened to you?

I found one of my friends — something terrible had happened to her. What? She had broken her doll, and she was sitting there on the curb crying, and I just stopped to help her. The mother said, What did you do, honey? How did you help her? I just sat on the curb beside her and cried with her. How profound that is.

That was helping her in her loneliness and sorrow. Just somebody to sit there and say, I cannot cure your loneliness — but I can sit here and cry with you. And when she did that, it let her friend quit crying, and it blessed her.

All around us are people who are lonely — they are crying — brokenhearted. You want to transform your loneliness by reaching out — by seeing them and saying,

119

Just let me sit on the curb beside you and show my love, and show my care. That transforms loneliness.

And then, the fourth way: *Sanctify your loneliness.* Let your loneliness bring you to God. Let your loneliness bring you to the one who made you to be lonely. He made a vacuum in you that He alone can fill, and you will never be satisfied and fulfilled until you let God come into that vacuum and fill it.

Augustine said we were made for God. And the nameless longing in every human heart — the ultimate loneliness — is this constant seeking and searching and waiting for that vacuum to be filled by God Himself. He made us that way. He made us for Himself, to belong to Him. Let your loneliness cause you to find God. Come to Him in prayer; open up your heart and say, Come in Lord. In so doing, your loneliness will be transformed.

Jesus said, You shall leave me, and I shall be alone; but, no — I will not be alone for God My Father is with me. Jesus did promise, "I will never leave thee. Lo, I am with thee always." And the word of God says, I will never forsake thee.

There is a place in your heart made by God for God. You can fill it with self, and with pity, and with arrogance, and with self-interest, and activities, and chemical drugs to treat the ailments and all of this — but it will never be filled, and you will never be satisfied until you fill it with God — through faith in Jesus Christ — His Son and our Savior — to whom we confess our sins — in whom we believe — and to whom we commit our lives.

Out of the loneliness of our hearts sing, "What a Friend We Have in Jesus." The Friend of all friends — the Friend who will come and fill the emptiness of your heart.

ANCHORS FOR LIFE'S STORMS

Acts 27:27-29; Hebrews 2:1-4, 6:19

President Carter issued a dramatic declaration of the steps that would be taken to try to save the old ship of state. It seems to have been drifting toward the rocks of chaos — spiraling inflation — and interest rates going to 18-20%. We are on uncharted seas, stormy seas, worldwide — what is going to happen? President Carter has taken some dramatic steps to hold the old ship off the rocks. And, likened unto the story, we have thrown out the anchors and prayed for the daylight to come out of the dark night that encompasses us.

That is the parallel story I want us to see because there is a lesson and truth in the word of God and in this simple story about the Apostle Paul. It expresses that which happens to us as we sail the seas of life. We encounter storms, the tides cause us to drift; the rocks are not far off and we need an anchor.

THE SITUATION

Paul, a prisoner, was on his way to Rome for trial. This ship out of Alexandria had picked him up and they had come to Crete. They had put in to a tiny harbor and the captain said, This is no place to winter — the sailors will get bored — poor provisions, and poor protection against the storms. The first fair day we will try to go around the point for harbor. Paul warned them, but the captain said, Yes! When the deceiving soft winds blew upon them, they set sail.

No sooner were they out of port than the dreaded northeast wind swept across that Mediterranean — as it can do in the winter months. The ship was tossed and driven across the face of the sea in rain and darkness. The sun did not shine — for 14 days they were swept like a derelict ship without control. On the 13th night the sailors heard in the distance the roar of waves, and said, Land is near — we hear the waves breaking on the rocks — we are going to be shipwrecked!! Some of them panicked and began to launch the lifeboats, jumping overboard to save themselves. Paul said, Do not do this. And he persuaded the captain to throw out four anchors — all they had on board. And the scripture says they waited for the light to break — for the darkness to end — and the storm to be gone, and prayed the anchors would hold.

DRIFTING

Now — tie that story in with what we read in Hebrews where Paul picks up this same figure of speech: For life — your life — my life — is like a little boat cast out upon the waters. Paul writes to these Hebrew Christians, Watch out — therefore, be careful. We ought to give more earnest heed to the gospel we have heard — listen! — pay attention! — abide by the gospel you have heard, lest at any time we should drift away from these things.

You see, there are strong currents that run through life. Whether we recognize it or not, our lives are in the grips of those currents moving us along.

Life is not a pool, landlocked, calm. Life is a never-ending tide sweeping, driving us, like a storm at sea. They tell us there are currents in the sea. It looks steady and calm, but there is a river that runs along the edge of our continent — on the East coast — they call it the Gulf Stream. It appears as a calm sea — but there is a tide,

122

and a current, carrying it along.

They tell us that jet streams are in the sky. We cannot see them — it looks like the sky is still. But there are giant streams of Arctic air that flow like rivers through the atmosphere. When that jet stream swings a little to the south or off to the east from its normal flow, it brings these terrible winters, such as we had some time ago.

So as in nature, so in life. There are currents, the streams of life that carry us along. We can look around us and see some of these streams that catch us up and carry us along.

Take the stream of the mass media and the entertainment stream. Go to the movies— look at the television screen — read the literature that is published today. Isn't there a current that is sweeping and swinging? Isn't there a tide? If we are not careful, we are just caught up — we ride with public opinion as it swings up and down.

Take the moral tone of a country, a people or a society. Doesn't it go to the depths —doesn't it swing? Look at what is happening to the attitude toward marriage, for example. Isn't there a tide, a current, that is sweeping a generation along — that says, Why even bother getting married—just live together —bear children without marriage? Why get married?

Look at family life. A family and a home can get caught up in a current if you just drift along. I counseled with a couple whose marriage, after 30 years, was now on the rocks. I said. What in the world happened to you? They answered, We don't know — we just drifted apart. Drifted apart! By drifting in that particular stream— we drift apart.

Paul says that is true in the spiritual life— as he talks to these Hebrew Christians. He says, It is not

123

enough just to be saved — it is not enough just to give your heart to Jesus Christ and then sit down on a pew and say, I'm saved — thank the Lord! If you stay like that, you will be caught up in a stream where you will drift away. There are strong currents in life that sweep us along and we are in their grip. Life is not a pool — calm and steady — it is a stream — a tide driving us along.

A river, a stream, never flows uphill — it always flows downhill. And if we drift in the streams that catch us up — whether the streams of public opinion — streams of acceptable morality — the streams of our own Christian life, church life — or the stream of marriage and home— if we just get in that stream and drift, the direction is down!

Paul is saying to these Hebrew Christians — Watch out! Drifting may be pleasurable, but it is dangerous and deadly! We sing that song, "Drifting down the river on a Sunday afternoon" — it may be fun but it is surely not safe.

What does that say to you and to me? If we are going to save ourselves from the rocks of destruction, *we have to take charge*. We have to do something with our life. We have to go against the stream. It takes the *daily discipline* of going against the stream.

We know that in *our national life*. They say the price of liberty is eternal vigilance. One generation cannot pass liberty on to the next; they must earn it. In one single generation, we can lose it if we just drift — for the drift of a political structure of the world is the drift toward slavery and dictatorship—toward the loss of freedom. This is always true. Unless you struggle and fight for freedom, you lose it.

And the drift in the spiritual and Christian life is always away from God. We must swim against the stream and resist the flesh, the world and the devil. Jesus said,

124

"Broad is the way that leadeth to destruction and many there are who go that way" — that is the way of drifting with the stream. But narrow is the way that leadeth to life and few there are who will pay the price to climb that steep and narrow way.

Many today have let the streams of influence around them take charge of their life — and they are just drifting along. Don't you think it is time to say, I am taking over my life? I will not be swept along — I will not let the currents of circumstances in life carry me — I am going to determine my destiny myself; I am going to make some decisions and commitments about my destiny. No more drifting!

THE STORMS OF LIFE

This is also the story of storms. We are like a boat cast upon the waters and drifting in the stream that would carry us to destinies where we should not go — in a world where storms befall all of us, Christian and non-Christian alike. Just because you are a child of God does not mean there will not be any storms in your life — and this comes as a surprise to some new Christians. You think that once I accept Christ and settle in my pew as a church member, in a Sunday school class — start studying my Bible — I will not have any more troubles or problems or temptations or storms. Not so. The storms break upon all of us alike — the storms of life come — just as the storm broke upon Paul — the special chosen one of God, the choice of God— called of God, sent of God, commissioned of God to be the great Paul, the writer of a portion of our New Testament. Think of that! The storm came upon Paul equally with all of these rough sailors — the storm broke upon all of them. Out of this storm, I see three simple observations to help us in the storms of life.

First of all, *do not lose your head.* Do not panic.

125

They heard the waves crashing on the far rocks and started to jump overboard to save themselves. They tried to launch the boats. Paul said, I have been this night with my God, the living God. He told me that all is well; not a soul shall be lost. Stay on board — don't panic.

We need that lesson from Paul. We need to spend that night with God — see Him on the throne at the time of the storm. God is on the throne when storms come. He has not abandoned this world because it is having a rough time. He has not left you because life is getting hard and complicated and difficult. *See Him* on the throne. *Know He is in charge* in this world and He is in charge of your life.

Dr. T. L. Holcomb was my pastor at the First Baptist Church in Oklahoma City, where I was converted as a nine-year-old boy. In the years to follow, Dr. Holcomb became executive secretary at the Sunday School Board. This is one precious story Dr. Holcomb shared when we were both at Windemere, our Baptist assembly in Missouri. I was speaking there and he was leading the Bible conference.

He said, Let me tell you of something from the days of depression — times were hard. Businessmen committed suicide because they had lost their fortunes. This was oil country and many oil fortunes were lost.

Dr. Holcomb said, One day a little lady, a member, came by the office, just desperate. They had nothing to eat and were at their rope's end. She had been a clerk in a store; her husband a bricklayer, but there was no work for there were no bricks; nobody was buying. The lady poured out her sense of frustration and fear. Dr. Holcomb opened the scripture and talked about God — about God being on the throne — God caring for his own — and he prayed. You have to put your life in the hand of God. He will see you through the storm.

126

Then he said, I know of one place that is doing some hiring — the man in charge is a member of our church. Go to this address tomorrow — it opens at nine o'clock — if they have an opening, you apply for it.

She went with hope in her heart. When she got there about 8:30 there was already a line of people waiting outside the door. When it opened at nine, she saw there were 40 or more people inside. She sat down and waited.

About eleven o'clock the little window opened; a man looked over the room and said, I'm sorry — we are not hiring today — there are no jobs.

A hush fell over the group as they started to leave, one by one. The lady was stunned — they had prayed about it surely, God was going to do something. God had let her down.

As she started to leave, the man, still standing in the window said, Lady, you wait. I want to see you. With all those people I didn't know what to say — we only have one job. I looked over the crowd and tried to pick out the person that seemed to fit the best; it looked like you were the right one. Fill out this form and we will see if you qualify.

She did qualify. She went to tell Dr. Holcomb — I go to work at three o'clock this afternoon in a cafeteria. I get some pay, and my husband and I will get a meal every day. You see, don't panic — God is on the throne.

In the storms of life, know He is there. Don't give up. Paul said it is not all over with — *don't lose your courage.* Be not afraid, he told those sailors. Have no fear — don't lose your courage.

The third thing he said to them: He preached to them. In the time of storm, *don't lose your opportunities.* What a time to be a Christian! What a time to tell what God can do for a person in the time of a storm.

These sailors probably had not listened to Paul before now. They were not interested in religion. But the storms came and, suddenly, they saw Paul had something they did not have — and he did not lose his opportunity to bear his witness. What a wonderful time it is to bear witness for Jesus Christ.

Drifting — take charge of your life — don't be swept along. The storms will come — but God is on His throne — don't lose your courage — don't lose your opportunity to bear your Christian witness. And then . . .

THE ANCHORS OF LIFE

The story tells us they threw the anchors out and waited for day—waiting for the light to break. Sometimes we just have to throw out the anchor — Lord, I am in darkness — I don't understand it — but I am waiting for more light. And He gives the light — and as we begin to understand, we begin to see. Paul picks up this same figure of speech, and I think it is significant.

Paul had experience with shipwreck when they threw out the anchors. Paul talks to these Hebrew Christians about drifting — don't be carried away like that.

Then, in Hebrews 6:19 — about Jesus Christ, he says: Which hope we have in Jesus Christ as an anchor, both sure and steadfast for us. The anchor of life is a vital personal faith in Jesus Christ. When you have that anchor on board, throw it over and you will not drift. The streams may run past you and carry others on down — but you can stay anchored, steadfast and sure; you will not be swept along. And when the storms break, you will not be driven onto the rocks of destruction. The anchor is Jesus Christ, Paul says.

So, what do we do? Let's get a vision of our life

128

committed to Jesus Christ — let's see what can really happen — what He can do, if we let Him have our life. Take charge of your life and turn it over to Him.

Some years ago, a little black boy came to Chattanooga, Tennessee, off a tenant farm in North Alabama. He went to a black church and sang in the choir. He had a beautiful voice. A doctor heard him and took him under his wing. He told him about Jesus Christ — about a personal commitment of his life to Christ and led him to make that commitment.

Then, he said, Son, you have a great voice — God has given you a rare gift. I want you to see what God can do with a man who has a voice like yours. I want you to hear a great singer, and he played some records of the great Caruso.

The boy began to get a dream — maybe God could take his life and talent. Out of that commitment came the great Roland Hayes, one of the greatest voices the world has ever known. He sang in the courts of the kings in Europe and on platforms throughout the world. He became a vigorous witness for Jesus Christ. And a great one on the forefront of Christian brotherhood and dispelling discrimination and racial hatred. He saw himself in the hand of God and trusted himself to God through Jesus Christ. He had a lot of storms — read his biography about the conflicts, the controversy, the bitterness that was heaped upon him. But through all of those storms, he had an anchor in Jesus Christ. So, see yourself committed. Then give yourself in service to Jesus Christ. That is the anchor.

Several years ago I heard Louis Evans, pastor of the First Presbyterian Church of Hollywood, California, tell about an experience on the mission field in Korea. He went to a Presbyterian hospital and the mission doctor asked if he would like to see a major operation. Dr. Evans said yes and he was directed to a balcony

129

which looked right down onto the operating table. For seven hours, in intense heat, the doctor operated, pausing only to refresh himself.

Finally, he was through. As he came out, the next patient was ready to roll in. Dr. Evans said, Aren't you through? No, this lady is ready to go in. Doctor, what would you get paid back home for an operation like that? Well, at least $500. What do you get here as a missionary doctor?

Dr. Evans looked at the waiting patient; she was holding a copper penny in her outstretched hand. The doctor said, All I want and all I get is her smile and the Master's approval — not any greater pay in the world than that.

That is what Paul is saying. When your life is anchored in Jesus Christ, in service to Him, His cause, and His church, day by day. It is a sure steadfast anchor that will hold you.

OVERCOMING SPIRITUAL

DISCOURAGEMENT

Romans 7:19-25

One question in a recent seminar discussion went this way: Can a person really change his life-style — that is, can you really get new values and stick by them, or will you fall back to your old life-style? Now I knew the context in which this question was asked — because this was a seminar of help for those who had been divorced. And someone in that group was asking the question that all of us ask in one area or another of our lives.

How can I conquer the physical drives within me — the animal instincts within me? Here is a person who has been married for many years; there is a certain pattern of physical expression through sex that is acceptable within marriage. Suddenly the marriage is broken, either by death or divorce and then comes this awful struggle — how can I control and keep submerged this drive within me? Even though I set my ideals high — can I really change?

The alcoholic says this, again and again. I will never take another drink. There is the goal and the ideal. Then, suddenly there comes moral failure and he is down again. Deep inside — whether he asks anybody else or not— he says, I wonder, can I really change?

There comes a moral and spiritual discouragement that becomes self-defeating. Our own self-image is destroyed as we look at ourselves and say: Is this me?

I don't like myself! I can keep up my front with others; I can make them think one thing — but I know what I am really like inside.

Now that is what the Apostle Paul was dealing with; you realized that from our scripture passage. Paul says, There is a war going on inside of me. The things I would do I do not. I set my goals. I pass my resolutions. I would do them, but I fail. And the things I do I really do not want to do. I blow up — I don't want to do that. And, yet, somehow, something inside me compels me to do it in certain circumstances.

So, Paul says, I have discovered a law. The law is this: There is sin — the law of sin is still in me. Though I am converted and saved, the old law of sin still works in me — the carnal man, the physical man. But, also, I have discovered a second law. There is the law of the Spirit that is in me, and these laws are at war.

Then Paul issues this desperate cry: Who shall deliver me from this body of death? I always thought that simply meant, Who shall deliver me from this physical body — this body that will die — this body that will go back to the dust? That is part of the truth in this statement — but I think there is a broader meaning and a deeper meaning than this.

In Paul's day there was a special punishment for the criminal who had committed murder. Instead of executing the criminal, they simply strapped the body of the victim to his back and he was to carry that body of death on his back until it rotted off. A horrible punishment — to go to bed at night with that terrible rotting thing strapped to his back. He would wake up in the morning and there it was; it smelled even worse. He would sit at the table to eat and the awesome stench would nauseate him. No one would come near him. Thus he lived with this terrible *body of death* strapped to him.

Now Paul says, That is what is strapped to me. It seems as if this body of sin — this old body of sin that was there when I was an unregenerated, unconverted person — is still strapped to me. How am I going to get rid of it? How can I get rid of it? Then with a shout of victory, he says, I thank God — it is through Jesus Christ that I will get rid of it!

And that is what we are dealing with as we talk about overcoming this spiritual discouragement that comes — when we have such high ambition and such low performance — when we aim for the stars and we hit the dust.

Now to a certain extent, this deals with what psychologists call our *self-image*. How do we see ourselves? And what are we really like? How do you see yourself?

I want us to look at ourselves in several different ways. First of all . . .

SEE OURSELVES AS WE ARE

We have to start realistically. We are not being realistic if we wear rose-colored glasses and say, Oh, there is nothing wrong with me — I am charming — I am successful — I am good-looking — I am a great person —There is nothing wrong; I don't need a thing.

Jesus said, The well need no physician. Now, you can keep up that kind of bold front to make everybody think you feel that way about yourself. But in your secret moments when you sit down and look yourself in the face — you say, there is something wrong inside me. I am like Paul. I know there is a battle inside me — something is wrong. And what is wrong with me is sin. I am shackled to it. I am the victim of it. I am made a captive of sin.

Of course, that is what the Bible tries to tell us

133

again and again. All have sinned and come short of the glory of God. There is none perfect, no, not one. All we like sheep have gone astray. Again and again, it tells us our righteousness — even the best we are and the best we can do — is as filthy rags in the sight of God. We have no worth in ourselves, of ourselves; there is nothing you and I can do to make ourselves acceptable to God. It is only through something happening to us through God's grace that we have any worth at all.

Did you ever stand in front of a mirror and look at yourself and suddenly say, Do I look like that? Do I really? Turn sideways — Do I look like that? That is when you say, I am going to diet — I am going to change — I didn't know I looked like that.

We must do that morally and spiritually — see ourselves as we really are and we start there. You cannot have a good self-image until first you have a bad self-image. You cannot become a child of God until, at first, you admit, I am a child of the flesh — I am a child of sin. I am undone — woe is me! That is where it starts — when we see ourselves as we really are — without God — without hope — without righteousness — lost— separated from God.

Then, the second vision we need is to . . .

SEE OURSELVES AS WE MAY BECOME

We are not locked in to what we are. That is the glorious good news of the gospel. You do not have to keep on being like you are! You can be changed! That is what the word *conversion* means. You can be converted. You can be going in this direction — something can happen — and it can turn you — and put you in an entirely opposite direction. Conversion means simply getting the devil and sin out of your life, and bringing Christ into your life and giving Him the key to every room in your life. That is what conversion is.

Jesus talked about conversion — being *born again*. He said to Nicodemus, You can be born again — you *must be born* again, or you will never see the kingdom of God. We need to see ourselves as converted persons — turned around.

See ourselves with a *new nature* inside us. Listen: I John 3:9 says: Whosoever is born of God doth not commit sin; for His *seed remaineth* in him: and he cannot sin, because he is born of God.

When you are converted and born again, God plants a new seed in you — *His seed in you* — and you become a child of God. You have the genes of God in you. Mark you, 2,000 years ago they were recognizing that there is a kind of continuity of characteristics and nature that is passed down in a bloodline. They just called it seed then. We call it genes today. The principle is still there. You now have the genes of God planted in you so that, as you grow and develop, you grow into the likeness of God — not into the likeness of the devil.

Now you say — I am a little troubled over that verse because that verse does spell out my problem. If I have the genes of God, the seed of God in me — and it says, If I have been born again and have that seed — I do not sin. Does that mean that if I sin, the seed of God is not in me? That seems to be a contradiction of everything I started out saying — doesn't it?

Here is the answer. The King James translation of the Greek is not exactly accurate. The Greek is such a finely shaded language, that one single Greek verb would take a whole sentence in English as it expresses tense and action. This verb, *doth not sin*, is a linear action, not a punctiliar action in the Greek.

Simply, here is what it means. Literally translated — whosoever is born of God and has the seed of God in

135

him — the genes of God in him — *he doth not keep on— and on —and on— and on, committing sin.* It does not say, *will not sin.* He does not keep on committing sin.

There are two levels. We are born into this world and only the seed of man, the seed of the flesh, the seed of sin, the seed of the devil, is in us. Here we are at this level. We are satisfied in our sin and loving our sin.

Then, one day, we are *born again, converted* — and brought up to a higher level above sin. The genes of God — the seed of God — put in us. Once we are up on this higher level — we are growing with the characteristics and the nature of God in our lives — we go along at this level.

Now, whosoever has *God in him* — he *does not keep on sinning.* It does not say he will not sin. He will drop down to sin — but he will not stay down there. The very fact that your conscience bothers you — the very fact that you say, Oh, why did I do this? — I don't want to be like this — I know I have disgraced myself — I have sinned against God and against others. The very fact that you have concern says that the seed of God is in you and you will not stay down there. You rise back up.

The illustration I like to use so often is the difference between a sheep and a pig. A pig gets in the mud and stays in the mud. You get him out of the mud, he will fall down and he will stay there. A sheep is above mud; he does not wallow in the mud puddle. He might fall into a mud puddle, but he will get back up because it is against his nature.

So it is. We get a new seed in us when we are born again and we are converted. We get *a new nature* inside us. And God makes out of us a new creation, the scripture says. See what God sees in you. He sees you converted. He sees you with a new nature with His seed, His genes planted in you, a child of God that will let you and make you grow into His likeness. You will sin and fall many times. But you are on your way up toward Him.

And He makes a *new creation* of you, a new being. Something entirely different than what you were before.

And then, the third vision is to ....

SEE OURSELVES AS GOD SEES US

This is the glorious vision we need! How does God look at you? How does God look at me? The glorious thing about God — He is not imprisoned with time and space. We see ourselves as we are in space and time right now and we say, I am a poor example — what a rotten Christian I am. What a miserable failure I am — I understand Paul— I am so discouraged.

But God sees us not where we are and as we are now; God sees us for what we can become out yonder. He is able to see beyond time and space. He sees what we shall be someday. And when He sees that, His approval is upon us.

See yourselves as God sees you and know that God believes in you. And if God believes in you, God cannot be wrong. Remember that! We know how much it means for somebody else to believe in us — what confidence, encouragement, strength and power it gives us when someone says, I believe in you! You can!

I heard about a professor, Dr. Floyd Baker, who taught physics for twenty years. Dr. Baker taught the only course in higher physics that was required for a major in that subject.

He was tough. When the new class came in every year he stood before them and said:

If you are trying to get a major in this subject, you had better pass this course — or change your major. You cannot get it without credit from me. If you cannot get along with me, you had better change your major. I am going to tell you what I expect of you. I do not like lazy people — I do not like people who will not study. I am going to give you the material and you are going to learn it. And I am going to pass you. But, if you don't learn it, you will fail. And 50% of the people who take this course fail. Don't you be in that 50%. With that he would stalk out of the room.

Dr. Baker said, He would sit around the faculty lounge and brag about how many failed his course. He thought that was the mark of a good professor — how many would flunk. He made it tough on them and laughed about it.

But, one day, I met Jesus Christ and had a personal experience with Him. I learned what it meant to be concerned and care about others — and try to encourage them instead of discourage them — try to bring success into lives instead of defeat and failure.

So he said, When Jesus changed me, I went a changed person before my class — and here is what I would say: This is an extremely difficult course. You have to study very hard in this course to pass it. And, you need to pass it to get your major in this field. But I want everyone of you to pass the course. I want to help you pass it.

Now, you do your part and I will do mine. I think working together we will see that not a single one of you fails this course this year. Let's work together on it. You can do it if you will try.

Dr. Baker said, The amazing thing is that my prediction came true. When I used to say 50% would fail, 50% did. When I said, You can do it — everyone of you— they did! I did not change my grading one bit. I did not change the content of the course one bit. I expected just as much of the students. They rose to the level of high performance when I told them they could and I would help them.

Do you realize if that can happen when a human being says, I believe in you, you have something in you worthy and worthwhile — and I will help you achieve the goal of your life — how much more so will it strengthen us and help us when *God says, I believe in you*. Think of it! From the very foundations of the world, I started planning on how to bring the best out of you!

Then, Jesus Christ believes in you. When he took up that cross and started to Calvary, He said, I am doing this because I believe the best in you. I believe you can be a child of God. That is what Jesus spent His ministry doing. How many times He helped people get a better self-image — to go away with their head up.

Remember Mary Magdalene who broke that precious ointment on Jesus while others said, Look at that prostitute. Wasting that ointment — look at her. She heard it. Jesus heard it and said, This dear woman shall be a memorial in history and her name shall be remembered forever because of the love she has shown for me. In other words, He pointed out the best in her and restored her self-respect. She has something fine in her and I am going to hold that up.

Remember Zaccheus, the traitor, who sold out his countrymen. Jesus said to him, There is a true son of Abraham. How he had longed to hear someone say, I accept you. Everybody else ostracized him. Jesus said, I will accept you — I will go home with you. A true son of Abraham.

Or the woman taken in the act of adultery. Jesus said, Where are your accusers? She said, They are all gone. He said, Neither do I condemn thee; go and sin no more. He gave her a new start, a new beginning, a new life.

God believes in you. Jesus believes in you. They cannot be wrong. Get your head up. Say with Paul, It is so wretched. I feel so miserable when I fall. But, praise God, through Jesus Christ, I can get on my feet and I can keep going on.

But you know, the longest journey of a thousand miles begins with the first step — at a definite time, at a definite place — when we take that step.

It is that simple to start on the Christian pilgrimage. You start by accepting Christ— by opening your heart — by receiving Him — by making a commitment of your life to Him, then moving on to grow as He plants His seed in you, and the genes of almighty God begin to work as you grow in His image.

If you have not made that commitment— will you make it?

A RELIGION THAT WORKS —

IN THE CRISES OF LIFE

Romans 8:28, 31-35, 37-39

This has been a week when the headlines have focused on the disasters of life. In Washington State, Mount St. Helens erupted, covering the countryside with hot volcanic ash — 18 people died and many more are still missing — millions of dollars worth of damage done. Weather in the whole western hemisphere was affected in the settling of this dust for two years. A great calamity — a natural disaster in that corner of our country!

And then, moving across the country to Miami, Florida, another disaster. A riot breaks out — 17 people are dead — over 200 injured — $100 million worth of property damage! Tempers run high and an explosive situation is there. A social disaster and crisis.

In between, the country is struggling with other kinds of disasters. The automobile industry is a shamble. The housing industry is at its lowest level in many years. Unemployment is rapidly rising. And we say, What comes next! What will we face? — not in natural disasters or social disasters somewhere else, but in personal disasters that confront us all in our daily lives: Sickness — death — loss of job — the shattering of dreams and hopes — the breakup of a marriage — all of these things that come upon us.

So, I want to talk about a religion that works in

the crises of life, when disaster comes. That is exactly what the Apostle Paul is talking about in this passage that we read from Romans 8 — the disasters that come upon us and shatter us in the twinkling of an eye, like a volcano erupting and entrapping us, like a violent riot that breaks around us, and circumstances beyond our control catch us up and carry us along.

And, as you read this full chapter, you can see how Paul, the teacher, begins to lay his premises, his concepts, and ideas, and build, step by step, to the conclusion — much like a geometry teacher writes a theorem on the board — draws an isosceles triangle and then begins to validate that theorem, to prove that theorem — and then spin off from that the corollaries, the next one and the next one. That is the process Paul is using here.

Vs. 31. He lays the base of the triangle — he states his theorem — God is on our side. Would you grant that? And if God is on our side, what shall we fear? If God be for us, who can be against us? That is the first premise. And he goes on to show us how we can prove that.

Vs. 32. Is not the death of Christ for us — dying on the cross? Isn't that evidence that God is for us? He that spareth not His own Son, but delivered Him up for us all, how shall He not with Him give us everything we need? There is the proof, the validation. And he goes to his next corollary.

Vs. 35. Paul says that the love of Christ, then, is our security. We find our strength and our assurance in the love of Christ; and it is so strong that nothing can separate us from that love of Christ.

Do you see how it has built up? If God be for us, who can be against us? We have nothing to fear. The proof of that: Christ died on the cross for us. God gave His Son to do that, won't He do everything else?

142

Therefore, if these two things are true; the third thing is true: The love of Christ is so strong that it can grasp us and hold us so tight that nothing can separate us from the love of Christ. And then . . .

Vs. 37 sums it all up. Nay, in all these things — things that come against us — that would try to separate us from God — we are more than conquerors!

Now, Paul was writing to the Christians in Rome; they knew about conquerors. The marching Roman legions went everywhere, conquering. The generals came back from their farflung battles bringing the trophies of victory.

Rome was accustomed to the parades to honor the conquerors. Here would come the generals who had won the battles in Africa, the Middle East, or yonder in Galatia, parading down the street on their white horses. Behind the generals would be the officers, then the soldiers marching with great pride. Then came the carts and servants carrying the booty, the wealth they had gathered up from the conquered peoples. Then, in chains and ropes, came the slaves — men, women and children. Rome was accustomed to seeing conquerors.

But Paul said, Through your faith in Jesus Christ, you can be a conqueror over all the enemies in life; yea, even more than a conqueror — greater than these conquerors whose victories are but for the moment. You will be conquerors forever!

In other words, you were born to win — you were not born to be a loser — you were not born to be defeated. You were not born to be overcome by the circumstances of life. When you are born again in Jesus Christ, His love, His power, His presence, come into you— grab hold of you and you are born again to win! To be a victor! To be more than a conqueror!

143

And then *the conclusion* of it is in vs. 38. For I am persuaded — that brings us to the conclusion — all of this proves that nothing can separate us from the love of God. I am persuaded that neither death, nor life, nor angels, nor principalities, nor powers, nor things present, nor things to come, nor height, nor depth, nor any other creature — he just cannot leave out anything; he covers every conceivable possible development of life — none of these shall be able to separate us from the love of God, which is in Christ Jesus our Lord. Born to win over these things! More than conquerors!

Well, if this is true, then let us draw some conclusions. Four very simple things I see here.

ACCEPT THE DISASTERS AS REAL

Paul says, Fellow Christian, *face the reality of life.* Do not minimize realities. People say, I'm a good Christian. Nothing is going to happen to me. Friends, you are wrong. You had better say, I am a good Christian and everything is liable to happen to me. Life is real. These enemies are real! You cannot take a Pollyanna faith that says everything is going to be rosy; I do not have to worry about a problem — because life is going to be full of problems. Paul spells them out. They are going to come after you — death, principalities, powers, nakedness, distress, persecution, all of these things. I faced them; you are liable to face them, too. So, let's not get that brand of Christianity that sticks its head in the sand and does not want to face life.

And let's try not *to run away from life either.* This is the most tragic solution — All around us are people trying to escape the realities of life. They will use any kind of narcotic, or alcohol; it insulates them against the reality of life for a short while.

144

We have a national disaster on our hands, medically, with 11 million alcoholics so dependent upon the crutch of alcohol that they cannot let it go. Most of them drink to escape reality, to escape the problems of life, the problems within their own heart or their own self-image and guilt, or their misshapen personality. They get a kick out of the alcohol that makes them feel like somebody they know they are not. When it is all over with, they come back down to face the reality of life; it is still there; nothing has changed. We have synthesized other kinds of drugs and chemicals to accomplish the same thing. We take millions and millions of tranquilizers every year, or hard drugs — trying to get away from the realities of life.

Now a Christian does not say, (1) it is not real; I will stick my head in the sand; or (2) I can escape it; I can take something and get away from it; I can run from it. But you cannot do it. The Christian says it is real and I will face it.

Foy Valentine, formerly with the Christian Life Commission, has a story he likes to tell. He was in a vulnerable spot as somewhat the conscience of Southern Baptists and, sometimes, he was so far out in front on the issues of life that he got under fire and attack.

Dr. Valentine tells about the fellow that went to the psychiatrist and said, Doc, I think I am getting paranoid. I look around and everything anybody does, I interpret as their being against me. I just can't get over this feeling that they are out to get me. The doctor finally said, I have examined you and I don't find any evidence of your being paranoid. The truth is, they really are out to get you.

Paul is saying, The forces of evil are out to get you; the evil in this world is real!

The second thing I would say. . .

KEEP LIFE FLOWING OUTWARD

The first step in trying to solve this problem then is to keep the movement of life flowing out from us. Don't turn in on yourselves. Don't smother yourselves with self-pity. This is the most disastrous thing we can do. It will destroy us if we begin to feel sorry for ourselves.

Why did this happen to me? I've been a good Christian all my life — I tithe — I go to church. And now, this sickness — now this loss — now this suffering. . . And so we think we are the only one that has ever suffered. Why did God pick on me and not somebody else? Keep the movement of life flowing outward. Don't fall into bitterness.

You see, a clean wound will heal. But if it is not clean, and becomes infected, it will not heal; it will fester, become worse and destroy the body itself. Now crises, tragedies and sorrows, and pain and suffering and death — all of these are as real as a knife cutting us. They cut us deeply, and we are wounded.

We cannot deny that life hurts us, but if we keep the wound clean from bitterness and self-pity, the wound will heal. We have to keep self-pity out of the way — keep bitterness out of the way — and keep life going outward from us.

Reader's Digest carried a story some years ago. A Mrs. William Wallace took her three boys to the doctor to get the shots required for school. As she and the boys — bright, husky, young boys entered the office, they saw a little girl on crutches with a withered leg. The girl said, Hello, I am so happy today — the doctor told me that I am going to be walking soon. He is going to put a brace on my leg and I can walk and run and play!

In a few minutes a woman came out of the office with a boy who had a twisted arm and withered shoulder. The

146

little girl jumped up and cried, Mommy. . . . Mrs. Wallace thought, Oh, no — you mean — God, did you do this? A mother — with two children like this! Surely not! She said she almost rebelled in her heart with bitterness — why would this happen?

As Mrs. Wallace went into the office, she said, Isn't that terrible — a mother with two children like that. The doctor said, Let me tell you something. Before you pass judgment, listen!

There was a young man whose parent was in a mental institution, with a mental disease. He went every Sunday afternoon to visit. There was a young women whose mother was in the same institution. She also had a mental disease. These two young people met each other and fell in love and married.

After they married, they came to me and asked a question.

Here is our history — these are our parents. If we have children, is there any possibility that we might pass this mental disability to them? We have compounded it, the two of us, by marrying. I told them the best I could of what I knew about it. They decided not to have children of their own.

They said, Doctor, would you help us adopt children? Of course, I said yes. But, they said, we don't want a normal, healthy child — we want you to find some little baby with a terrible handicap that nobody else wants and nobody will take — get it for us. We want one that is handicapped because we know what it is to be handicapped. We want to love them and give them what they need.

So, the doctor continued, I found the little girl — but they found the boy themselves. They are two of the most wonderful parents you have ever known — raising two of the finest children you will ever see anywhere.

147

They are going to be a great man and woman, these two are!

You say, Why? Because they kept the flow of life going outward. They did not say, Oh, God, why did you do this to us? They did not become bitter. They said we will give — we will pour out. That is the second principle here.

First, the enemies are real. Second, keep the movement of life flowing outward. Third . . .

HOW TO OVERCOME

Don't be concerned over why it happened. Paul does not say anything about why these things happen to us. That is not the point. Paul says the point is *how can I get power to handle* these things? Having an answer does not help me at all.

So many times people say, Tell me — why in the world did this happen to me? I can't — but how would that help you? I think it would help me just to know why! *How* would it help you? Could you handle it any better if you knew why it happened? They say, I guess not.

You see, *God gives us what we need.* We do not need answers, intellectually, we need strength inside us. Paul says that inner strength is what God gives us through Jesus Christ.

A woman was told that she was dying of cancer and it was incurable. The first word she said to her husband and to her doctor — Well, that's it. All right. Pray for me — and everyone thought she would say, Pray for me that God will cure me, that I will be delivered. But — no! She said, Pray for me that I might set an example before my two sisters and my brother — they are not Christians. Let them see what it means to be a Christian and to die like a Christian.

You see, she was not trying to find out why; she was saying there is power in me through Jesus Christ that can give me the Victory — and I want others to see that power in my life!

So, don't seek an answer; just reach out and take hold of that power — lay hold on that hand that has hold on you. Claim that love that has claimed you. Paul says none of these things can separate us from the love of Christ that is holding onto us.

So the fourth step is . . .

TIE ON TO THAT TRUTH

His love is sufficient. Tie onto it! It is adequate to hold you — tie on to it. Don't tie on to the things you don't understand— tie on to the things that you do understand in your Christian faith.

I say this to young preachers at the seminary — don't get up and preach about the things that you do not understand, the doubts that you have. You can preach a lifetime on the things you do understand about the gospel — and that is what we ought to do.

So, with our faith, let us lay hold on that which we do understand — and Paul says we can understand this: If God be for us, who can be against us? We know this. We understand this, because Christ died on the cross for us.

And if He died on the cross for us, we can understand that His love — that was great enough to sacrifice His own Son for us — that love is so great that it can hold onto us, and we can never be separated from that love.

So, where do we wind up? God loves you. That is the greatest verse in the Bible: For God *so loved* the world — and so loved you — that He gave *His only begotten Son*, that if you believe upon Him, you should not perish, but you would have everlasting life.

That is what we hold on to — and that is the kind of religion that counts — a religion that will work in the crises of life.

Do you have that kind of religion — that kind of faith?

ANTIDOTE FOR ANXIETY

Romans 8:28, 31-32, 35, 37

The woman was long-faced, and seemed to have a dark cloud on her face, when a friend asked her, Aren't you feeling good today? Oh, I feel good today. But — when I feel good I always feel bad because I know it is downhill from now on and, sooner or later, I will feel worse.

We laugh at that — yet, that is a very accurate expression of what we call anxiety — whether it is conscious or subconscious. Even when a person is feeling good, there is still this dark cloud of subconscious apprehension — anxiety — a fear of the future — the anticipation of the worst that will come. It is living under a cloud all the time. It is like a fog that presses upon us.

Psychologists call it free floating anxiety. And none of us are immune — it affects all ages — in all circumstances. A child can have great anxiety that affects all outward expressions of life — tension in the home — anxiety about security — father and mother arguing — fighting — adolescence — anxiety about the future — uncertainty about the ability and capacity to handle life — the demands made upon them — the pressures. Marriage can be afflicted by anxiety and old age. It has many expressions — outward symptoms and evidences of anxiety, from knots in the stomach to perspiration and hyperventilation. It affects us physically — it is a contributor to heart trouble, to heart disease, stomach ulcers — mental breakdowns and even suicide. Anxiety defined basically and fundamentally as apprehension — fear of what is going to happen — always anticipation of the worst.

How is it treated? There is the *medical treatment* of anxiety with drugs — the oldest known drug to the Western World being alcohol. The simplest way to solve the problem of anxiety is an injection of a drug. For a time, you are free of the cloud that hangs over you, somehow you can live the life that seems unbearable without the drug — you live awhile.

Or, there is the *psychological treatment of anxiety*. Sometimes, in severe cases, the only solution is to tranquilize the anxiety in order to understand the root of the anxiety — the guilt that may be there — the experiences of yesterday that lie deeply hidden within us — that cloud today and blot out the sun of happiness and joy and fulfillment.

There is a third antidote which is so basic to all of us: The spiritual antidote for anxiety. It is only when we have the right relationship with God and the right understanding of God and His nature that we can live today and face tomorrow without anxiety or fear or apprehension. Only a genuine valid faith in God — an experience that links our life with His — can give us the ultimate antidote for anxiety and apprehension about the future. That is where I want us to start. I want us to talk about this antidote.

The Apostle Paul gives it to us in a single verse: We know that all things work together for the good of them that love God, of them that are called according to His purpose. He does not say, we hope — we believe — we desire — that all things are working for the good. We *know.* This is a certainty that can be ours. When we can latch onto this certainty and make it our own, then the apprehension and anxiety about tomorrow begins to fade into nothingness.

So, let us examine this proposition — this antidote. There are three things that Paul says here — three things for us to lay hold on.

First of all, *God works.* God *is* at work in this world. The great Creator and Sustainer of this universe — the one that some call the great mind — the first cause — the source of energy from whence comes all of life — that God is not an absentee God somewhere out yonder in the universe, abandoning His creation. He is not an abstract God. He is a God that is still in this world. He is in the act of creation. He is still dealing with His creation. He is still at work in this world. That is the first concept.

We can look around and believe and know that every event, every circumstance, is within the framework of God's knowledge and God's activity. That does not mean that He is the maker of bad and the maker of disaster — it means that He is in this world with all that is going on in the world.

Let me tell you the story of a boy named Freddie. He grew up in a British military family, living on army posts around the world. His father and his grandfather were officers in the British army. Freddie's three elder brothers were also commissioned as officers in the British army. So here was his dream — his life's ambition — to follow this pattern to be an officer in the British army and make his name in battle on foreign fields.

He went through preparatory school and college and applied for his commission — but it did not come. He waited and he waited and he waited. His life was aimless — he could not find the direction to go while he waited on the commission.

During that time a strange thing happened. One night his little dog had a barking fit and created all kinds of disturbance. That particular night, however, one of the neighbors whose daughter was very ill became irritated by the barking. She knocked on the door and

153

asked the young man to please do something about his dog. The barking was upsetting the sick daughter. And he very politely shushed the dog. And this started a friendship. She invited the young man over and he soon became great friends with the family.

This Christian woman took an interest in this young man. As he expressed his frustrations about the commission she said, Maybe God does not want you to be an officer in the army. Maybe God is calling you to the Christian ministry. Finally, he accepted her counsel. I will enter that open door — I will enroll at Oxford for the ministry. And five days after he enrolled at Oxford, his commission came through and he faced a choice. Everything within him wanted to be an officer, a military man — but he said, No. God was not in it. And little Freddie stayed at Oxford and finished in the ministry. He became pastor of a church and for 13 years he preached. And then, at 37 he died.

But, his sermons were published and distributed throughout the world. Frederick H. Robertson was hailed as the greatest preacher of the 19th century. He was called by the Church of England the greatest preacher they had ever had in their history. He was called the greatest moral preacher of that century for both Europe and America. His sermons and his influence have spilled over till this day. In homiletics, they study the preaching of Frederick W. Robertson. He was called the greatest orator of his day. Only 13 years — and that is what happened.

Now I want to ask you: Was it by chance that a dog barked at the moon one night and would not quit barking? Was it by chance that that very night the little neighbor girl was sick and the mother became irritated by the barking dog? Was it by chance that the manner of the mother calling upon a neighbor with a complaint — instead of angering the young man — formed a friendship whereby she could influence the young man's life?

Was it by chance that, in spite of the influence of a grandfather, a father and three brothers, as officers in the army, a commission for a younger brother was somehow lost on this desk and put aside on that desk and delayed month after month after month until it came five days too late to put this boy in the army? Would you say that all of these circumstances were just by chance? No. It was by the providence of God.

God is in this world, and God is at work in His world today. You are not here by chance. You are not just the victim of blind fate — the thing that happened was a little accident that changed the course of your plans. God is at work. He is all around us in everything that happens. He is in this world at work. That is the first step in the antidote for anxiety.

The second step: *God works for good.* He has the power and the capacity to manipulate the events of life for the good. Now it does not say that everything is good. There are bad things that happen to good people; there are good things that happen to bad people; there are some good things that happen to you and me as Christians; and we take the good things that God gives us and pervert them and make bad things out of them. I have known people that God blessed with money — they were good people — God's people — but that blessing became a curse in the way they misused it and the way it captured them. So, it is not saying that everything is good. It says that God is able to take all the things that happen and *work them together for good.*

It was a bad day when Joseph's brothers became jealous, and angry and resentful of him and threw him into a pit and, finally, sold him into slavery in Egypt. It was a bad day when Joseph was thrown in prison by the accusation of Potiphar's wife. It was bad days on bad days on bad days.

155

But one day, when he had become prime minister in Egypt, his old father came with his brothers because of famine throughout the land. Joseph says to his brothers, You planned it for bad when you sold me into slavery, but God has worked it for good that many might be saved. All of these things God worked together for the good. That is what is happening in our lives. God can take even the bad things that happen and dovetail them and fit them together to make them come out good.

Let me tell you about Mary Verghese. She was born in South India and, through many hard struggles, set a goal to get an education. She did at Vellore College, and then went on to medical school and graduated as a surgeon with honors. For two years Mary Verghese practiced medicine. A Christian doctor in a land that desperately needed doctors, she ministered to her own people in the name of Christ.

But one day Mary was in a terrible automobile accident that left her completely paralyzed from her arms down — she only had movement with her arms and her head. A poor hopeless cripple — a brilliant career destroyed— that was a bad thing that happened. But God can take all the bad things of life and put them together and, somehow, make them come out good.

Mary took her accident and her crippled condition in stride. I am still a doctor. Her friends said, But you cannot practice. Yes, I am going to be a doctor. She voluntarily prescribed for herself three major operations. Those operations were to freeze her back and her legs so her body would be locked in a sitting position instead of lying flat on her back. She came out sitting in a wheelchair, rigid and locked in that position for the rest of I her life; but her hands were free so she could move herself about.

Now — I am going back to medical school to be a surgeon for the lepers of India. I have read about a

French surgeon who is doing marvelous things with muscles, nerves and tendons in the hands of people, and in their feet. I am going to learn this surgery. When you have leprosy it cripples and deforms. It makes rigid stiff claws of people's hands. I am going to learn how to be a hand surgeon and restore the use of hands and feet to the leper. She became a pioneer in the field in which Dr. Kleinert and the hand surgeons of Louisville are now this world's specialists.

Mary Verghese began a brilliant career of service sitting in her wheelchair beside the operating table as she made a crippled hand or foot whole. She rolled through the corridors of the hospital and patients said, Why, she is more crippled than I will ever be — if she can do this, I can do something with my life, too. Her life became a blessing and benediction to thousands of people — because a God, who is at work in this world today, was able to take even the worst of circumstances and work them together for the good. God works — God works for good!

And God works for good for us. Not just for the Apostle Paul — not just for Joseph in the Old Testament — not just for a lady doctor yonder in India — but He is working for you and for me today. That is the promise.

Paul says, How do you know that? He who gave His Son so freely to die on the cross for us — He who gave His Son to save us from our sins, individually and personally — won't He, because of that, give us everything in life? If you believe in a personal salvation of an individual — if you believe that we are personally saved by Christ's death on the cross — that Christ personally died for you and for me — and that we can come to Him as the Son on the cross and personally receive our salvation in Him — then we have to believe in the personal Providence of God. If He would do that for us, won't He come into our redeemed saved lives and

157

be personally involved and do for us that which is best and right and good?

So — here is the antidote. Paul says, I have no fear of the future. What can separate me from the love of God? Peril — misfortune — hunger — disaster — anything? The future is not a black wave of uncertainty sweeping over me. Anxiety cannot engulf me because I have this kind of personal faith and personal God who is in this world. He works — He works for good — He works for good for me!

But notice— *there is a condition*. Some people stop right there. . . .For good to them that love God, to them that are called according to His purpose. This is not a blanket promise to everybody. It is a promise *to those who are inside the center of God's will* with their lives. You cannot rebel against God — you cannot be disobedient — you cannot be outside His will and say everything is going to be all right. You ought to have a lot of anxiety if you are outside the will of God — that is what ought to make you anxious. But if you are inside the will of God with your life, that is the antidote.

You may have heard this story but I tell it again. When we moved to Birmingham with three small children — to a pastorium one block off Bessemer Highway — at that time called bloody Bessemer — the most heavily traveled highway in Dixie at that time — I was anxious about them. We had a fence around our backyard — and I put a chain and lock on the gate so it could not be opened. Inside the fence, I made it grassy and put a sandbox, swings and everything. The only way you could get in and out of it was to come through the house.

Then I took the three children out there and said to them: This is where you are to play — you are not to get out of the yard — it is safe inside here — I have picked up all the glass and nails and made it nice and safe for you here. But if you climb over the fence and get outside, there are mean dogs down that alley — they bite you— there are nails in that alley — if you step on a nail we have to take you to the doctor and get shots. There is glass that will cut your feet. If you go further down there outside this fence, there are cars that are going to run over you and crush you. Outside the fence terrible things are going to happen. But you stay inside the fence and I have made it safe for you.

That is exactly what God is saying. God works — God works for good — God works for good for us — who are inside the fence! But — if you are going to climb over that fence and get outside and say, I know I am outside the will of God — I know I am disobedient — I know I am not living right — I know I have not surrendered myself to Him — I know I do not belong to Him completely — I am holding onto some of my life— then some terrible things can happen — and they will not be for the good.

How do you get inside the fence? It is so simple and so easy, although we make a hard thing of it. Jesus said, Behold, I stand at the door and knock. Let me use an illustration so simple but you will have to use your imagination. Imagine that you have an old house up here on the river. You bought an old rundown farmhouse for your summer recreation place — a place where you can get away from it all. Nobody has lived in it for a long time, but it will be a great cabin — a good fishing cabin — a good place to go. Last Fall you boarded it up — you nailed boards over the windows — you locked the door — you shut it up tight.

This Spring morning you go to open up the house. Inside it smells musty and dingy — cobwebs are everywhere — it is dark and gloomy. You have to get this opened up and aired out — get some fresh air and light in here. Do you take a bucket, go outside and get

159

buckets of daylight and sunshine to carry inside? Do you go out and say, Fresh air, come into this house here. Fresh air, I need you inside. No. You just open up the windows, swing open the door and the air comes gushing in, and the sunshine floods in, of course.

Jesus says, Your life is a house, and it has a door. I am at the door knocking. If you want me to come in — what do you have to do? If any man will get his life straightened out and start to church — no. If any man will straighten up and fly right — no. If any man will read the Bible, know all about it and understand it — no.

Jesus says, If any man will *open the door....* Open up your heart — open up your mind — let Him come in. It is that simple. We make such a hard thing of letting God have our lives and it is so simple. You do not recite a creed — you do not have to know all the scripture — you do not have to go through all the rituals.

You just say, Lord Jesus, come in. Swing open the door and like sunshine and fresh air, Jesus Christ comes in. When He comes in and fills your life, out the door goes the darkness, the musty old fears, the darkness of anxiety, the clouds that cause us apprehension and anxiety about tomorrow, as the light comes in. He lives in us — and we can say, God works for good for us in this world.

Some of us need to climb back over the fence and get inside the will of God. We need to do something about our church membership. We need to do something about baptism, or rededication of our lives. You know you ought to do it — and God is saying, Get inside the fence so I can give you that freedom from apprehension and that antidote for anxiety and that deliverance from failure.

He wants to give that to you today.

160

STRENGTH FOR TROUBLED TIMES

Ephesians 3:14-21

These are troubled times, internationally, nationally, personally. And that is what the Apostle Paul is writing about in this book he sent to the church at Ephesus.

The passage we read has two magnificent words that just leap out at us. First, the word, *strength*, and then the word, *power*. No words could be more relevant for our day than these two words — as relevant as the headlines of the morning paper. Strength and power! The need of this day is for strength and for power.

President Reagan said that the Soviets, the Communists, understand only strength. And, unless we have strength greater than their strength, they are going to take the world.

There is trouble in South America and Central America. Trouble in the Middle East. Trouble in Poland. Trouble in Afghanistan. He says we must cut everything else in the economy — cut it back — but not military spending, because we must be strong to meet these troubled days in world affairs.

So, when we talk about strength for troubled times we are talking about something very relevant — and when we talk about power — the power that is in you and me. Isn't it a power shortage we are facing today? The word, energy, is a more sophisticated word for power. We are seeking more energy somewhere else — oil is running out and getting excessively high — atomic energy

— nuclear energy — solar energy — thermal energy. We need strength — we need power— we need energy for the troubled times of this day.

I think maybe that is why we are so fascinated by strong persons, and why we are so fascinated by even the little images that we conjure up of strong people — like the fantasies we have on television of Superman. We all watch Superman and say, Look how strong he is. Or Spider Man even. Or the bionic man or the bionic woman. They even have a bionic dog now. Stronger than any of the rest. And I guess the greatest fantasy is the Incredible Hulk.

So, we watch, fascinated, saying, Look at the strength — look at the power of this person in overcoming all obstacles in life — and we fantasize ourselves into being able to be strong enough to do that.

But, you know, that is not the solution to our problem. We are not called upon to outrun locomotives or jump over high buildings. The real battle we face is the battle inside; there is where real struggle takes place. The battle against depression and discouragement — the battle inside against sin and the erosion of faith as it begins to collapse under the pressures of a troubled world. We need some kind of power and strength, inside — and that is exactly what Paul is writing about here.

He says, I pray that you might be *strengthened in the inner man* by God's spirit — strengthened inside — the conquest of inner space, not outer space. We can put as many pieces of hardware as we want out yonder in space; it will not solve our real problems. The real problems rest in inner space — inside the heart of man. We need strength, and achievement, and victory, and power.

Then, a little further down, Paul talks about the

162

STRENGTH FOR TROUBLED TIMES

power *that works within us.* Not the power that is generated out there in a nuclear reactor to light our homes. We need some kind of a generator going inside us that gives us power and strength that will solve the problems of life.

So — this beautiful passage is a prayer, really. Paul has two prayers in Ephesians — and it is significant that we contrast the two prayers. Turn back to Chapter One — he has a prayer. And then in Chapter Three, he has a prayer. They go side by side, step by step; and they go from lower to higher.

In Chapter One he talks about the revelation of God; in Chapter Three, the realization of God. In Chapter One he speaks of spiritual enlightenment; in Chapter Three, of spiritual enablement. He talks in Chapter One, that ye may know — in Chapter Three, that ye may be that which you know. Chapter Three is the fulfillment and action of the knowledge of Chapter One.

In Chapter One he talks about light; in Chapter Three, he talks about life. In Chapter One, he talks about how to *know* the power of God; in Chapter Three, he talks about *experiencing* the power of God. In Chapter One he talks about the power of God working for us; in Chapter Three he speaks of the power of God working in us. In Chapter One, he talks about *you in Christ*; in Chapter Three, he talks about *Christ in you.* It is a marvelous parallel between these two chapters. We move from the knowledge and theoretical acceptance of our faith in our minds — to the enablement and enactment of it in us and out of us.

I find three magnificent figures of speech, or images, for us. First, the picture of a house; then, the picture of an athlete; and a third picture of a tree. If you can pray the three prayers attached to these three images, you will be on your way to discovering the secret of strength for troubled times.

THE HOUSE

First — Paul says, I pray that *Christ may dwell in your heart by faith.* (17). Christ may dwell — *katoikeo* is the Greek word. It means that Christ may come into your heart to live. No, more than that! It is more than just moving in to rent or to abide, or to be the guest. In the country, we used to see the little sign, Christ is the unseen guest in this home. It is not talking about guests, visitor, renter. The word in the Greek literally means *He will come in as the possessor and owner of the house.* That Christ may take up abode, and live in the house of your heart.

It is the figure of speech that you are a house with many rooms — and Christ wants to come in and live throughout the house — in every room. There is not a secret closet that you have kept for yourself — where you have hidden the skeletons of secret sin in the past, or the present lust and love. It is the complete ownership and occupancy, holding the deed and title to the whole of your life — the total commitment of your house to Him — that God moves in and takes over. That is the first step — the beginning point, Paul says, of discovering strength for troubled times.

Now — have you let Him into every room? Does He really abide, and own, and possess you in the realm of your business, in the realm of your pleasures, in the realm of your love life, in the realm of your social activities — how about it?

Or, are you claiming just to let Him have that spiritual religious room there — the chapel of your life? And the rest of your life, you are going to let other things of the world possess you, own you, and live in those rooms.

Paul furthers this figure of speech as he mixes it —

164

STRENGTH FOR TROUBLED TIMES

to dwell in the *house of your heart.* Your Christian faith is a matter of intelligence, certainly. It is a matter of the head. It is important to have a theology that undergirds your faith, or a doctrine that undergirds your faith. Doctrine is like the skeleton of a body; without a skeleton, it is all jelly. It would have no form and could not hold its shape.

But the skeleton without meat is dead. And a religious faith that is just the intellectual skeleton of faith is dead also. So it is not a question of how orthodox you are, how sound theologically you are, or how intellectually satisfying your faith is to you. It is not a matter of just saying this is the plan of salvation and, intellectually, I accept it. I think we reduce salvation down to this kind of simple statement: I am a sinner — I believe that. Christ died for my sins — I believe that. And I do accept Jesus Christ as my Savior. Then you are saved — that is true; that is the outline, the skeleton. But you cannot say, I have said that — I have recited it — I have completed it — intellectually, I have accepted it — and so, I am now a Christian and I can live as I please and do as I please.

Christ can dwell in your head that way. But the Bible says, Out of the heart come the issues of life. Surely, out of the heart comes the commitment of life. So Christ must dwell — not just in your head — but in your heart!

A friend of mine pictures it this way. A minister kept going to a lady's door asking a strange question. The lady would come to the door; he would say, Excuse me, does Jesus Christ live here? The woman taken aback by such a question stammered and said, No, and slammed the door.

And he came again. Does Jesus Christ live here? He came again and again and again, asking the same strange question. And, then, one day — when he

165

knocked and asked, Does Jesus Christ live here? — she said, Yes, I have come to understand what you mean. He *does* live in our hearts and in our lives — in this family and in this house. Jesus does live here. Paul says that is the starting point.

Help for troubled times? Man, how can you face these times without Jesus Christ? Does He live in your heart? Does He?

If He does not, I would not go out of this room today without saying, I need Him — I must have Him — I cannot face another day, another minute, without Him! I need Him!

If He does abide in your heart, throw your head back, and say, He is here in my heart and I can face the world!

Paul moves on to the second figure of speech.

THE ATHLETE

He picks the figure of an athlete. I pray that ye may *be strengthened with* might by His spirit in the inner man. (16) The word, *strengthened*, is an athletic figure. The athlete goes into training — exercising and exercising — making himself strong. Yonder in the field house at the University of Louisville, spring practice is under way. Those men are already lifting weights, and going through all kinds of physical exercises — not playing the game of football— but they are disciplining themselves by rigorous rules of training and hard exercise so they will grow bigger, stronger, heavier— so they can fight the battles of the football game this Fall.

Paul says there are spiritual disciplines, too. You cannot just say, Praise the Lord, I have opened my heart and let Jesus in — I am saved! — and sit down on a pew. I can be lazy the rest of my life — just do nothing

166

about it — I am heaven bound — and I can just sit there and grow a strong Christian life. You cannot do it without exercise — *spiritual exercise.*

The *exercise of prayers.* It is an exercise — a way in which we come to know God more thoroughly and intimately.

Faith is an exercise. The more we use our faith, the stronger our faith becomes. The less we use our faith— as with my arm if I bind it up — the weaker it will become until it is limp with atrophy.

So faith and prayer, the gathering of ourselves together for *worship,* and the *reading of the word of God_*— all of these are spiritual exercises. The scripture says, Forsake not the assembling of yourselves together. Wonder why so many people are weak and unhappy in their Christian life — miserable, day by day? They have drifted apart and drifted away. They have forsaken the gathering together. They have forsaken worship. They are forsaking the love of the brethren, the study of the word of God — and corporate prayer together — this sort of thing.

Paul says, I pray that you may add to this figure of a house — the house of your heart — with Christ dwelling in it — and the figure of an athlete — exercise every day — so that in the times when there are no stresses and strains and conflicts, you are building strength for the day when the test of a hard time comes. Just as there can be no strong athletes developed by breaking the rules of training — there can be no spiritual giants built by breaking the rules of spiritual training and discipline.

Some of you need to make a new commitment to your church. You need to be in Bible study in a Sunday school class. You need to get back to reading and studying the word of God. You need to come back to some disciplines. That is a part of the secret of strength for troubled times.

Then the third beautiful figure of speech . . .

THE TREE

Paul says, I pray that ye may be *rooted* and *grounded* in love. (17b) Rooted and grounded like a tree. When hunting in the Big Horn mountains of Wyoming, we saw the windfalls where these tall scraggly pine trees, covering a whole mountainside, had just blown down. The trees had fallen over like matchsticks, or dominoes, toppled over. What has happened there? It looks like devastation unimaginable came through here. We were told, Those are ridgepole pines — tall slender pines and the first heavy winter storm that comes will knock them down like that — they are so shallow rooted. Other trees are not blown down — they are deep-rooted.

The same is true in Christian lives. I see Christian lives just topple and collapse because they do not have real roots. The storm comes and they fall over.

Paul is saying, Like a tree, be rooted. Run your roots deep into the ground. I know lives that are grounded in sensuality — lives that are grounded in physical appetites, in pride, in self-fulfillment — just in sheer selfishness — lives that are grounded in business, in money — all of these groundings will not hold the roots of your life. When the storm comes, the trees are going to collapse, I promise you.

Paul says to ground yourself in the deep soil of love — the love of Christ which passeth all understanding. The word, *passeth*, in the Greek means, *overrun*. This love of Christ goes beyond the understanding of men. The length, the breadth of it, the height, the depth of it is beyond our understanding and comprehension. Root yourself in the love of God. Stand back and say, How much He loves me!

In the last century a young French priest by the name of Joseph Damien came from France at 23 years of age and buried himself in a prison of misery on the island of Molokai, Hawaii. Bound by a rock cliff 2,000 feet high and a level plain about three miles long and a mile and a half wide, the island was skirted by a dangerous beach and reef, and 1500 lepers lived there. This lone man came as a missionary to live among them.

You saw the documentary on his life on television, maybe. He built houses for them saying, Wasn't the Savior a carpenter?

He built a school and brought in books and taught them to read. Wasn't the Savior a teacher?

And then he built a hospital and brought medicine. Wasn't the Savior the great physician? Finally, he built a chapel, and another, until he had five chapels on that island for these poor desperate lepers. Wasn't the Savior the Son of God?

In one of those chapels some years later, Father Damien made one of the most dramatic and profound statements a man has ever made in the service of our Lord. He stood in that pulpit and said: Fellow lepers, we are now one in body and in soul! And they gasped — for he was saying, I now have your disease — having lived among you, touched you and loved you — now I am contaminated, too. And a short time later, he died of leprosy, so disfigured, a horrible death. But one of his last words was, God is so good — my work is finished — I am no longer needed— I can go home to be with Him.

You say, What a story! A man who went — and lived among lepers — then to die of their disease!

That is what Jesus did. He came down to live among us to take our disease of sin — and take it into His own body and to die for us. And it is finished!

169

WHEN LIFE GOES TO PIECES

When we contemplate how much He loved us, we have to say, If He loved me this much, He will surely never, never forsake me. In that love I root my life, knowing that He will, as Paul said, do exceeding abundantly above all that we ask or think, according to the power that worketh in us.

May you claim that power through faith in Jesus Christ through fellowship in His church.

WINNERS AND LOSERS —

What's the Difference?

Philippians 1:12-18

Two top basketball teams, Indiana and Marquette, played an exciting game. When the game was finished, one was a winner and the other was a loser. Now — what's the difference?

Sydney J. Harris, the syndicated columnist, wrote a book on this subject in which he points out some of the differences between winners and losers. Let me read a few:

"When a winner makes a mistake, he says, 'I was wrong'; when a loser makes a mistake, he says, 'It wasn't my fault.'

"A winner respects those who are superior to him, and tries to learn something from them; a loser resents those who are superior to him, and tries to find chinks in their armor.

"A winner takes a big problem and separates it into smaller parts so that it can be more easily manipulated; a loser takes a lot of little problems and rolls them together until they are unsolvable.

"A loser becomes bitter when he's behind, and careless when he is ahead; a winner keeps his equilibrium no matter which position he happens to find himself in." Interesting observations!

Life is a game to be played, a race to be run — a battle to be fought. Paul spoke of this many times. And there are winners and there are the losers.

God has planted in all of us the instinct to be winners. The psychologist says something like this: The strongest human urge is the urge to excel, to achieve, to overcome, to master the situations of life. A fundamental human characteristic that pulls together many motives and drives is this one characteristic, to be a winner — a success — to achieve. That is a God-given instinct!

It is rooted in the Old Testament, for we read in Genesis that God created man in His own image — for man to play the role of God. In other words, He put something of God in us. We are to subdue, to conquer and use this world that He made. That instinct is found only in humans!

Now — we find around us many pressures and drives to help us — to push us to be winners. The very culture we live in spurs us to success. The pressures of society. What does the business world say to man? Listen, you've got to cut it or you can't stay with us. You've got to produce. You must be a winner all the time or we cannot use you!

We as parents put this kind of pressure on our children to achieve and excel. I want you to be at the top of your class — to make the team — to be the best. To achieve socially, and morally. You must be a winner!

The young wife says to her husband, I want you to make your mark. Why don't you do like so and so? She spurs him on.

He comes home and says to her, You be a good mother, a good housekeeper. You are supposed to manage this home!

There is pressure from society— formulas on how to be a success in life. How to achieve. Look over any rack of paperbacks. The publishers saturate the market telling us how to be a success; whether it is Napoleon Hill's book on *Think and Grow Rich*, or Dale Carnegie's book on how to achieve in social relationships, or how to make a million dollars in real estate.

One interesting formula was a mail order success program. There was a big sign with the word SUCCESS on it. Stick this on the bathroom mirror in front of your eyes, and every morning, stand three feet away and look at it intently. Place your right hand on the back of your head, slowly bring it over your head to point directly at the word, and say, I am a success! I am a success! Do this five minutes every morning.

We laugh at this — yet there is validity in all of these ideas on how we should have the right mental attitude. Of course, Dr. Peale's book, *The Power of Positive Thinking*, is one that has motivated many people to turn from negative thinking, to get their lives in order and set goals.

I have preached many times on the value of enthusiasm, of positive attitudes, of goals and goal setting. And I am not demeaning in any way the value here — but something really stunned me.

While we have this motivation and drive to succeed — and all of these people want to help us to be a success — I realized that not everybody is a winner! Not everybody can be, or will be, successful in everything they do. When the basketball season is over, only one team can be the winner. There will be scores of losers. It's hard to be a loser! I recall how we boys would find a great pile of dirt and play "king of the mountain." We got into a fight to see who could climb to the top and stay there by keeping the others down. There could be only one king of the mountain; everybody else was a loser.

So it is in life. For every man who gets to the top— there are thousands who do not make it. The hard

173

reality of life is, there are few, if any, who have continuing success in every way. It is an impossibility to be a success every time, in every venture, in school, in athletics, in the social life, in the business life, in the moral life. Who can say, I've never failed! The truth of the matter is that life is a mixture of success and of failure. And most of us have more failures than successes.

Now — if you have never failed, if you have reached every goal you have set in life, if you have lived up to every ideal in life, if you have never known a disappointment, if you have never made a mistake, I do not have anything to say to you. You can just tune me out.

But — if you, as I have, missed the mark and fallen short — while I have achieved some things, I have failed in many others — then I have something to say to you. I want to talk about how to be a failure. Nobody tells us how to cope with our failures. You start out with dreams, ideals and goals — and then you do not reach them! You are lost! Defeated! You are a failure! What are you going to do? Let's look at it.

HOW TO BE A FAILURE

How to cope with and handle the disappointments of life, the mistakes of life, the failures of life. Let's lay down a couple of premises.

First of all, *beware of a false sense of failure.* Let's be sure we *have failed* before we say we *are a failure.* An inferiority complex is in those persons who imagine they have failed when they really have not. Many times we think we have failed when it is really not failure. We compare ourselves to the wrong people or the wrong thing.

For example, a young boy who plays quarterback

on the high school team is a state All-Star. The hottest boy in high school football! He is really good! He has made it! He is a success!

But suppose he compares himself with one of the offensive backfield men of the Miami Dolphins who is a professional football player. Alongside this skilled giant he thinks, I'm a failure! I can't run like he can, and I can't pass— I can't make yardage like he can. I'm not as strong as he is! He talks himself into a failure. Because he is comparing himself to the wrong person. The wrong ideal for comparison.

This frequently happens between fathers and sons. The son idolizes his father; he wants to be more like him. As he tries, and compares himself to his father, there builds up in him a tremendous sense of failure — and hostility, resentment, conflict resulting in a terrible inferiority complex. The boy did not know his father when he was his age. He did not know how inadequate and limited his skills were. Much heartbreak and misunderstanding and tension develops because we compare ourselves to the wrong thing or person, and say we are a failure!

A second premise: *We really must face up to our failures.* Do not run away from them by excusing yourself. It wasn't my fault anyway — I'll try something else — it was the circumstance — the setting — the people involved. The poet said, If I had the wings of a dove, I'd fly away and find peace. Every time you encounter difficulty and defeat and discouragement, you just fly away to another situation. Change jobs. Change situations. Change environment. This will not help you; you have to face it. If you fly away, you take your failure with you. It is inside you. What you need is a change of attitude and heart inside.

So — the second premise — we are going to stand; we are going to face it. Yes, I have failed. I have messed

175

things up. Yes, I have fallen short. It's me. I want to know what to do about it! Now — how to cope with failure!

FAILURE IS RELATIVE TO PERSPECTIVE

How you look at it. There is an old Norwegian tale about a fisherman and his two sons who were out on their regular run when a terrible storm came up. The winds were so strong and the wave wanted to just swallow the small boat. They lost their direction. Eventually, though, they made their way safely to shore.

In the meantime, on shore the strong winds had blown into the kitchen fire of the fisherman's hut — higher and larger until the shack was on fire. The wife tried in vain to put out the fire, but the house burned and every earthly possession they owned was lost. As the boat landed, the tearful wife cried in agony, Carl, I have bad news — our house has burned down; we have lost everything. He seemed unmoved by this and said nothing. She said, Don't you understand me, Carl, we have nothing left. We have been wiped out.

He said, Let me tell you what happened to us. The storm came up, we were lost; we didn't know which way to go. The wind was so strong. But then we saw a tiny orange light. It grew larger as we pulled toward the light. Your husband and your two sons were saved, for it was the fire of our burning house that saved us.

It is perspective — how you look at it. On this side it may look like disaster and defeat. But, over here, it was a glowing success!

And that is what the Apostle Paul is saying in Philippians. Here I am, a minister of the gospel, a missionary. I intended to come and preach to you in Macedonia, here at Philippi. I intended to come to Jerusalem. I intended to go to Rome and preach there — what happened? I was defeated! I was in a riot in Jerusalem. I was arrested, and put in jail. I was imprisoned at Caesarea for two years. I was sent on a ship but the ship wrecked on the way to Rome. I suffered many hardships.

Now, I am in Rome and still in chains. You say these are defeats — but they are not defeats! All these things have happened for the furtherance of the gospel.

In my preaching in chains, I have strengthened the brethren. They preach with much courage here in Rome. The whole guard has been converted, even Caesar's household. People inside the army have been converted. I see God's hand on it for success, not defeat. Some say I have been defeated — but I say it is all to the furtherance of the gospel.

This is what Paul means in Romans 8: All things work together for the good of them that love God — of them that are called according to His purpose. In other words, when we get God's perspective — our life is in the hands of God — we are living as best we can to understand and do the will of God in our life — then, God takes things like the burning of a house, which is bad, and turns it around and uses it so it ultimately becomes good. The imprisonment of Paul, the beatings and the chains of Paul, bad in themselves, fit together in a pattern that makes them good!

So — the first thing I say to you— don't pass judgment — don't be despondent — don't get down on yourself and on others saying, I have suffered defeat —I have failed. Because it is really relative to perspective. If your life is in the hand of God, you have an assurance that God is with you. As for God's perspective, He has the power to make all things fit together for right.

FAILURE IS RELATIVE

TO THE RIGHT USE

Among some articles Deacon Ed Hampton had given

me I found this motto: "So you have failed—how fortunate you are. Now you know what not to do." That is right! In other words, failure is good or bad according to the use we make of it. If we learn from it, learn what not to do—all of science is predicated on this. Laboratory work is discovering a thousand ways something will not work so we can discover the one way it will work.

Even Eve and Pierre Curie worked in the laboratory trying to find that fleeting substance — they did not know what it was that was radioactive. And they did not know what radioactive was. They searched and searched. The biographer says, Pierre said to Eve, We'll never find it — in a hundred years we'll never find whatever it is. And, of course, they discovered that radioactive substance, the whole principle of radioactive elements that is the basis for the cure of cancer today. You see, it was only when they failed and failed and failed that they finally found it. It is the use you make of the failure — whether you learn from failure. What are you learning? What do you now know?

What kind of motivation has it given you? Are you ready to say, I'll keep on and on and on? Or, I'll quit! What if Paul had quit the first time he was imprisoned? Nobody wants to hear me preach, they threw me in jail. He was in prison many times. He was beaten and left for dead. What if Paul had quit when he was first shipwrecked? What if Peter had quit when he denied the Lord? I failed him, I'll just quit.

What if Jesus Christ Himself had quit when He failed in the first sermon He preached in Nazareth — in His own synagogue? The people became so angry with Him, they took Him outside and threatened to throw Him down a cliff and stone Him to death. What if He had said, Nobody wants to hear me — my own people turned their back on me— my own hometown? What if

178

He had quit?

You see, failure is relative. It is failure only if we let it be failure. If we let it be a stepping-stone to higher things — learn from it—stay with it —perseverance—commitment — and even further, if we let it bring us closer to God— in our dependence upon Him. Sooner or later, we all must come to the place where we say I can't cut it by myself. I need something — there is more to life than what I have. Oh, God, help me. That is turning the discouragement, despair and futility into success and victory. One man said, The greatest thing that ever happened to me was when life went to pieces. Only then did I realize how badly I needed God.

Failure is relative to our perspective. Failure is relative to the use we make of it.

FAILURE IS RELATIVE TO THE CHRISTIAN INTERPRETATION OF IT

... Even as success is relative to the Christian interpretation of it. The Christian interpretation of life says that it is not what I *have*, but what I *am* that is important. The great achievement of life is not what I can gather together to hold in my hand, but what I can develop of myself in character and Christlikeness.

We are made in the image of God. We are made to belong to God. We are made to be His. The greatest success in life is measured in spiritual terms. The greatest failure in life is the spiritual failure of life — to miss God— to miss His will— to miss His purpose for life. Everyone of us is planted here for a purpose to fulfill. We must pursue it with the same kind of diligence that we pursue other ends in life if we are going to find that purpose.

That is why Jesus said, The road is narrow — it is hard. You must seek it. The broad, easy way is the way to destruction and the way to failure.

But, the way to be a winner is the narrow way. You must choose it. You must decide on it. You must follow it. You must pursue it.

And it begins by a commitment of your life to Jesus Christ — receiving Him as Lord and Saviour, saying, My life is yours! I don't know all that means — but I want to give myself to you. I want to live for you. I will walk this path and pursue it.

WHEN FEARS FRUSTRATE

II Timothy 1:3-7

Today, fear stalks our nation, as on Three Mile Island at Harrisburg, Pennsylvania, a nuclear reactor is about to explode. Goldsboro is evacuated — the streets are empty. Pregnant women have been moved from a ten-mile area around this nuclear plant. Children are gone and a nation, yea, even a world, watches in fear about what could happen. Though scientists tell us it is a remote possibility — a very distant, slim possibility, nevertheless, fear grips us — fear of what could happen, fear of the unknown. What happens if there is a meltdown — if clouds of radioactive steam scatter out over this nation? Will it touch you — touch me? Will it affect unborn generations? Fear has gripped us; some say an almost irrational fear.

Perhaps we need the words of Henry Thoreau who said something like this: Nothing is so much to be feared as fear. President Franklin Roosevelt, speaking words of encouragement to a paralyzed and frightened nation said, We have nothing to fear but fear itself!

Biologists say fear is the oldest human instinct. Psychologists tell us we are born with two instinctive fears. The baby is afraid of falling and afraid of loud noises. As a child grows older, fears accumulate either from experience or from expanded knowledge. As an adult our fears have compounded until, at last, we are afraid of everything with which life surrounds us. We are afraid of life itself. We are afraid and worried about security. We are afraid of losing health, wealth, friends, position, face. We are afraid of failure.

NOT ALL FEAR IS BAD

Now — If fear is our common enemy — the nemesis of every man that walks the face of this earth — let us not make the mistake and say, Get rid of all of our fears. For fear, sometimes of itself and in itself, is not always bad. Fear is planted in the heart of every creature by God as an instinct to help us meet the dangers of life — for life is dangerous — it is full of accidents; it is full of mishaps.

A rabbit still lives today and is not extinct because God planted in his heart fear, his only defense. That rabbit can bound across the field with lightning speed on a moment's notice — because of fear. The adrenalin glands begin to pump into the muscles extra energy.

The deer is defenseless, except for fear. And the deer that cannot bound from an afternoon sleep straight into the air ten feet, land on all four legs, pumping immediately at maximum speed — that deer will not survive in a woods full of wildcats or dogs.

There are things we ought to fear. We teach our children to be afraid of matches. We want them to be afraid of old, rusty razor blades. We want them to be afraid of cars on the street. And we tell them what will happen to them if they get into the street in front of those cars whizzing by.

In society we must have laws and penalties and punishment. We have to implant fear in the hearts of people to make them do right. I do not agree with this philosophy that we should do away with penalties, and that fear is not a proper motive for doing right. You cannot induce everyone by love and good will to do right. Do away with jails and do away with laws — oh, no. It is the fear of penalty and punishment that prevents

182

us from doing wrong many times; yea, even the fear of death. I cannot agree with criminologists who say the fear of death in the electric chair is not a deterrent to crime.

Here is a very practical example. Speaking to you who are good, honest, decent Christians and church members: In a few days you are going to write out a check and send it to the IRS. Now, I ask you: Why do you write that check and send it before midnight, April 15? Because you just like to send checks to Washington? You just like to pay taxes? — You just love the government so? You want to give them all you have? Of course not! —You are afraid not to! If you don't, you will be penalized financially. You might even be put in jail!

So you see, fear has its place in the structure of orderly society. Fear has its place in our lives. The problem comes when fears are not rational. They become irrational and they dominate us and paralyze us. They cause us to lose our capacities and our power. That is when fears become bad for us.

The irrational fears we face are many. A leading psychologist said this: There are 20 million Americans who are obsessed with some kind of phobia. And they have clearly identified more than 700 phobias, all the way from acrophobia, the fear of heights, to zoophobia which is the fear of animals.

For example, there is an electrician, 34 years old, that has a fear of elevators. For all his working years, he has climbed 17 stories by the steps every day to go to work! Or the housewife who has not been out of her home in 12 years because she is afraid of open spaces. The psychologist says these are deep-seated fears. They are irrational fears. They damage and destroy us and limit us.

183

And then we all have temporary irrational fears — and how they limit us. We had a great big raw-boned 260 pound football player in this pulpit some time back just to give a one-minute testimony. He stood here shaking like a leaf — sweat on his brow — hands quivering and in a very timid soft voice he managed to get some words out. Now he could plunge into a line and tear them up on the football field — absolutely fearless physically. But when he stood before a crowd to speak he was terrified. That is an irrational fear.

I have seen this in so many weddings. I ought not to do this— the Lord'll forgive me and I guess you will. I was in the wedding party of one of our members, John Y. Brown, in New York, when he and Phyllis were married. He stood in front of Dr. Peale shaking like a leaf. And was so terrified that he could not even repeat the vows after Dr. Peale. He stuttered and stammered and could not get it out — and finally Dr. Peale gave up and said, That is a pretty hard phrase, let's just skip it. Then when he went to put the ring on Phyllis' finger, he could not get it on and she had to put it on. Now — that is an irrational fear. We all have them, but they pass away.

Then we have those continuing irrational fears that harass us and stay with us. They become buried deep inside us and become anxieties that cause us to be sleepless and toss at night, cause us to overeat, overindulge, overwork, overachieve. There are tensions in our relationships with family, friends and fellowworkers. We are on edge. These are rooted in subconscious anxieties and, subconsciously, these fears work on us.

God does not want us to live in this kind of irrational fear. Paul said, For God hath not given us the spirit of fear. He wants us to seize life and move forward with all of our capacities and abilities. God wants to give us three gifts: the gift of power, of love, and of a sound mind.

MANAGING OUR FEARS

I want to offer five simple suggestions on how to master and how to manage your fears.

First of all, get *your fears out in the open* — out in front of you. Write them down. Look them squarely in the face. Talk to yourself about your fears — talk to your loved ones. When you have ripped the mask from your fears, you will find they really are not valid; they are not rational. So, get them out of the dark. Don't suppress them into the basements of the subconscious where they will fester and create all of the anxieties that will cripple you. Get them out — look at them.

I will share a personal story of a fear I had — when I was scared to death. I was pastor at Rogersville, Tennessee. We had a smaller auditorium but much like this one. The pastor's study opened directly onto the platform.

One night about ten o'clock, I was in my study when I heard thump — thump — thump— someone walking with a heavy foot in that sanctuary. Cold chills went up and down my spine — my hair stood on end — my heart began to race — what will I do? I was too proud to call the police and too ashamed to run and admit to myself I was scared. So I decided to bluff my way and scare that fellow out of there.

The light switch was right by the door that swung out into the sanctuary. I turned the light on — swung open that door and yelled, Get out — I know you are there — get out! I'll call the police. Nothing happened. Nobody moved. I did not hear him breaking for the window or the door. I did not see a thing. Don't hide now — get out before I call the police! I'll give you two

185

minutes to get out. I closed the door. I did not hear a thing.

I decided to wait. I turned the lock on the door, incidentally. In a few minutes, thump — thump — thump! I thought I'd better take action. I got the poker in one hand and a heavy brass paperweight in the other hand. I slowly opened the door — talking all the time. You'd better get out now — wherever you are — whoever you are — get out! I couldn't see him or hear him. I looked around every pillar. I was halfway up the middle aisle and, suddenly, right behind me — thump! — thump! I was paralyzed! When I did turn around, I didn't see a thing. Then I looked down— right beside me was a friendly dog! As he walked under those pews, his tail would bang the back of the pew! I was as weak as a kitten. Then I began to laugh. How ridiculous! Scared to death — of this!

You see, as long as my fears were in the dark and unknown, I was terrified, paralyzed. They wrecked me. But when I got them into the light — looked them in the face—how foolish, how ridiculous. That is the first thing we must do — get our fears out and look at them.

Second— *analyze your fears*. Why? What is the nature of my fear? Many fears are rooted in our own ego. We are afraid of failure — afraid of embarrass-ment — afraid of the image. That is not logical. It is not what others think of us that is important; it is the esteem we have for ourselves that is important. Is our fear rooted in an irrational egotism that won't let us be ourselves — be open and have our own self-identity and self-respect?

How many of our fears are rooted in our selfishness — our own self-interest? What will happen to me? I am at the center of my fears. We are afraid we will lose— my resources — my health —my relationships. Focus on

186

self.

We need to say, Really, I must get out of myself —
it is not right to live a self-centered life. Only as I begin
to be anxious about others and their needs do I begin to
lose myself and quit worrying about myself.

Third: *Pray about your fears.* Come to God and
honestly say, Lord, this is what I am afraid of. I'm
scared to death. I want you to help me. Now, I know
some of you would say, That sounds like a preacher
now — just pray about it. That doesn't do any good.

I heard the story of the Baptist preacher who was
up in the Maine woods hunting bear. He found a bear
and it started after him. He began to run and dropped
his gun. The bear caught up with him and was about to
eat him up. The Baptist preacher didn't know what to
do but pray. Lord, Lord, make a Christian out of this
bear. Sure enough, the Lord heard his prayer. The bear
stopped, folded his paws, looked up to heaven and said,
Lord, make us thankful for that which we are about to
receive!

Let me tell you how to pray about your fears and
anxieties. Listen: It is the prayer of a woman who was
in a terrible automobile accident. As it turned out, she
was crippled and in a wheelchair. But she prayed:
Lord, you know I would like to walk. Give the doctors
wisdom and judgment. Lord, I pray for this one thing.
Lord, give me the courage to face up to life and be able
to be victorious in it. The Lord answered that prayer.
He gave her victory. I saw her in later years,
triumphant, victorious, bright, outgoing, a tremendous
influence. People loved her, respected her.

I know people who have prayed for all kinds of
things. They prayed for wealth and they did not get it.
They prayed for health and they lost it. They prayed
for this to work out and it didn't. Now God always

hears our prayers and answers, yes or no — I believe that. Sometimes He says no to these prayers. But I have never yet known a person who prayed to God: Lord, give me courage and strength to face life, but that God did not answer that prayer. He will give you the answer, if you pray. Take your troubles and your fears out — lay them before the Lord. Pray about them.

Fourth: *Use your fears,* Use them to stimulate you to action just like fear stimulates that rabbit and the deer to their best performance. That is the legitimate use of fear. If you are afraid of loneliness, don't sit around in anxiety because you are lonely. Let that stimulate you to give love away to people. You will find that gets love and friendship coming back to you. If you are afraid of bad health and sickness, go to the doctor and let him examine you; then take his word for what he says. Don't worry about it. Look ahead. Let it discipline you. If you are afraid of bad health tomorrow, discipline yourself today in the habits that will affect your health. Let fear stimulate you to action.

Then, finally: *Put your life in the hand of God in faith and trust.* This Easter season we are going to talk about what God has done for us through Jesus Christ on the cross.

There is a beautiful story about an Indian tribe that had the custom of sacrificing a beautiful maiden each year to the god of the river. They would put the maiden in a canoe and she would go to her death over the waterfall as a sacrifice.

The maiden was chosen each year by lot. One year the daughter of the chief was chosen. The day came for the sacrifice of the chief's daughter to be made. They led her down the banks of the river to the canoe. The chief was nowhere to be seen. The tribe said, He is a coward, he is afraid. He can come down when others are in this boat — but when his own daughter is to be put in the canoe, he is a coward.

They put her in the canoe and pushed it out into the current. Only then did they see, from the other side, another canoe putting out. As it came closer, they saw it was the chief himself. He made his way to the other canoe. As he came up to the side he grabbed the gunnel and pulled the canoes together. Then he reached out his hand and clasped her hand and rode over the waterfall with her.

That is the glorious good news of Easter. That is what God has done in Jesus Christ. From the other side of the river, He has come through His Son, Jesus Christ. That Son came to live among us, to die on the cross, to be resurrected the third day. He comes to take our hand and ride the waters, the stormy currents of life, at our side, and to go with us, yea, even over the falls of death itself to bring us safely out.

That is the Christian message. That is what God wants to give you today — the certainty of your faith as you respond to him. Listen to what Paul says: Stir up the gift of God in you. Timothy, stir it up. It is like a fire that has grown cold. There is only a little bit of spark left. But you stir up that fire and get it blazing again. If it is just a little bit of faith you have, act on that faith.

You don't have full faith. You don't have great faith — you don't understand it all. But you do have deep in your heart, a simple fire of faith burning.

There is a God — I know deep down inside. I believe God cares. And God loves. He is in this world. I believe He expressed himself through Jesus Christ. Stir that up, Timothy.

Let that faith burn in your heart. God does not want you to have the spirit of fear in your life; but of power, and of love, and of a sound mind. That can be yours, today, with a personal commitment of your life to Jesus Christ — by stirring up that fire. Just say, I am here, I want to make my life count. I do have faith in my heart. I do have faith in Jesus Christ as my Saviour — I do believe on Him. I do trust Him.

Would you make that commitment now?